URBAN GOVERNANCE IN NORTH EASTERN REGION

(Legal Issues and Practices)

U.B. SINGH

GYAN PUBLISHING HOUSE
New Delhi-110002

URBAN GOVERNANCE IN NORTH EASTERN REGION
(Legal Issues and Practices)
[*Administration, Management*]

ISBN: 81-212-0661-8

Published in 1999 in India by
Gyan Publishing House
5, Ansari Road
New Delhi 110 002

Laser Typeset at Alphabet, Delhi
Printed at Chawla Offset Printers, New Delhi.

Contents

Preface

The Constitution 74th (Amendment) Act, 1992 is a landmark in the history of urban local governance in the country. The enactment applies to all the areas except the states covered under the Fifth and Sixth Schedules of the Constitution. The North-Eastern Region comprising the seven states and Sikkim has a unique combination of administrative structure. In addition to the Fifth and Sixth Schedules and certain special Articles of the Constitution, the local administration in the region is carried out under the traditional primitive system besides modern municipal organizations. This widens the scope of interest among all the concerned.

The present volume discusses at length the modern municipal governance in its post-Amendment era. It is supplemented by a thorough study of the prevailing administrative system under autonomous councils. This is probably a pioneer work on urban local governance in the region and would necessarily provide a framework to the policy makers to bring uniformity in urban administrative system all over the country. Such a venture would also help in linking the North-Eastern Region to the national mainstream.

In completing the work I got assistance and encouragement from various corners. At the outset, I would like to place on record my gratitude to Messrs L.C. Borbarua, Dy. Director of Municipal Administration, Assam, L. Mohendra Singh, Asstt. Executive Officer, Tripura and M. Bhattacharjee, formerly Administrator of Agartala Municipality for providing respective Municipal Acts and to Sri B.K. Panda, Director of Meghalaya Urban Development Agency, Shillong for sharing the Act and dealing with District Autonomous Councils. I am thankful to Devendra and Soumendra for helping in finalizing the manuscript. I am thankful to M/s Gyan Publishing House, New Delhi for publishing the volume in record time.

Basant Panchami,
1999

U.B. SINGH

ONE

Introduction

The North-Eastern region of India comprises of the seven states of Assam, Arunachal Pradesh, Manipur, Meghalaya, Mizoram, Nagaland, and Tripura. The complex physiographic conditions proved restrictive to a large-scale urban development in the region in the past. Often described as a microcosm of the Indian subcontinent, the North-East is represented by all three physiographic divisions of the country, though on much smaller scale, the northern mountains, the central plain and the southern plateau.

As per the census of 1991, the region has a total geographical area of 2.55 lakh sq. kms. constituting about 7.7 per cent of the total area of the country and population of 31.5 million which forms 6.89 per cent of the country's total population. The area of the region was one-fifteenth of the country and the population accounted for 4 per cent of the whole in 1971. At the beginning of the present century, the population of this was 4.27 million. It increased to 10.26 million in 1951 and 31.55 in 1991. Thus, during the past four decades (1951-91) the population went up by more than three times. Among the seven states of the region, Assam's share is the largest being 71 per cent, followed by Tripura with 8.70 per cent, according to the 1991 census.

North-East India has a high concentration of tribal population. Excepting the valley, the region is inhabited by numerous tribes. Each tribe is an atomized group and is characterized by a nearly total absence of secondary intercourse with others. It proves that the region has remained relatively isolated from the influence of the cultures and civilizations of the Indian subcontinent for relatively longer periods of time in its history. The only common bond between various tribes of the region is administrative in effect. For purposes of development in these states, a joint action in matters of common interest was felt and the establishment of the North-Eastern Council was an articulation of this urge towards an integrated development of the region.

The sparseness of the population may be explained by the geography of this region. The countryside is mountain locked and the terrain is uneven. It was not until 1826 that this region could be said to have been firmly integrated, politically and administratively, with the rest of India. Yet the British interest in the region remained more anthropologic than administrative, even more academic than integrative till the end of their rule and the region was a latecomer into the national mainstream. As a consequence, the region has failed to generate the necessary objective conditions for the emergence of urban centres in the region.

The absence of large economic activities has cast its shadow on the trend of urbanization as well. The degree of urbanization in all the states was much below the national average by the year 1961. Meghalaya was the only state with a substantial proportion of its population, around 15.3 per cent, living in towns. The people in Arunachal Pradesh were entirely rural in their composition. However, Manipur had a semblance of urbanization, where about 8.7 per cent of the population enjoyed urban living. The level of urbanization in Tripura was only marginally higher than that of Assam. In Mizoram, only one out of twenty persons opted for urban living during 1961.

The level of urbanization picked up a higher pitch during 1981-1991 decade. The degree of urbanization showed an impressive upswing in Manipur too, though on a less dramatic note than that seen in Mizoram. Nagaland and Arunachal Pradesh too are experiencing greater urbanization in recent years. It is significant, though, that the level of urbanization remains stagnant in Meghalaya, Assam and Tripura, now although these three States recorded a relatively higher level of urbanization by the year 1961.

Interestingly, the higher elevations of the region are experiencing unprecedented urban growth and are fast outpacing the level of urbanization found in the states dominated by plains and plateaus. Despite having a large proportion of plain areas, the degree of urbanization in Assam remains incredibly low and its growth has been negligible during the past three decades. Likewise, in the case of Meghalaya, which has the largest share of urban population in the entire North-East, now occupies much lower rank and the urban growth was only marginal in the past three decades (Nayak). Urban development in the Nagaland hill tracts is confined to the low altitude foot-hill zone. The process of urbanization in the North-East seems to have been restricted to the administrative centres and the valleys in the hilly areas. In the Brahmaputra valley, the process of urbanization is yet to take off in areas with a large concentration of tribal population.

The structure of urbanization as revealed from the pattern of distribution of towns and population in different size-classes is inconsistent. The 1991 census recognized as many as eight cities in the region, supporting a population over a lakh. That a very large proportion of the urban population lives in large townships is clear from the fact that nearly two out of five urbanites (38.29 per cent) are claimed by these towns. The Class-II towns are, however, few in comparison and account for a little over 9 per cent of the urbanites in the North-East. Towns having population of 20,000 to 50,000 are far more numerous and support close to a quarter, around 23.2 per cent, of the urban population. Predictably, nearly all the large towns are located in the valleys and in the Meghalaya plateau. Assam has four Class-I towns while Tripura, Meghalaya, Manipur and Mizoram claim one each. Barring three of these towns in Assam, the remaining are the state capitals (Nayak).

Significantly, the annual exponential population growth rate in the region has always been found to be much higher (2.24 per cent per annum during 1901-1991) than the national average (1.18 per cent per annum). The total growth rate in the region during 1901-91 has been 638 per cent as against the country's average of 255 per cent. Among the states of the region, Tripura exhibits the highest growth rate of 1491 per cent, followed by Nagaland with 1091 per cent and Mizoram (737 per cent). Meghalaya records a relatively lower percentage growth (421 per cent) in the region, but still is higher by one and a half times than the national growth percentage. In the case of Manipur and Assam, the growth percentage is more than two times the national average while in Arunachal Pradesh, the growth has been more than one and a half times during 1961–1991 than that of the country's average.

The topography and the associated subsistent or quasi-subsistence nature of the economy have been the most severe constraints on urban development in the hills and the plateaus. The vast length of the valley in relation to the breadth hardly offers good sites. Despite the constraints imposed by the physical environment and the socio-economic structures, the region, of late, is experiencing large proliferation in the number of towns and increase in the proportion of people living in urban areas. These changes are, however, not accompanied by any significant and perceptible shift in the economic organization. Moreover, the level and growth of urbanization reveals striking regional variations with its concomitant implications for the region's overall growth and development (Nayak). While literacy percentages compare well with the all-India averages, the growth of urbanization is quite poor uniformly in all the states and territories when projected against an all-India perspective. The region is marked by a far higher growth rate of population during this century as compared to the other parts of the country. While the growth rate varies from state to state, in some cases, for example, Nagaland, it is more than double the growth rate of the country. This alarmingly high growth rate of population has a great impact not only on its geographic character but also on its socio-economic structure.

The economy of the North-East, when exposed to the modernization process, can be treated as rudimentary in form and self-sufficient in character. But tribal economy could be described as even more primitive than the economy of the people of the plains. For instance, even at the low level of economic development, an economy can be self-sufficient, it is only indicative that wants and needs were less than the supply potential of the economy. The limited wants of clothing, housing and food, could be met by the families on their own. Recently, the Government of India declared a package of economic development for the region, although its impact is long awaited.

Statutory Provisions

The heterogeneity in population and complexity in topography, unevenness in urban growth, tribal dominance and primitive culture have kept the region in an isolated state of economy and development, distanced from the national mainstream. The situation, therefore, led to the special status to the region in the Constitution of the country. A major part of the region is characterized as Scheduled Areas and special provisions have been incorporated for its administration.

The Constitution provides that the provisions of the Fifth Schedule apply to the administration and control of the Scheduled Areas and Scheduled Tribes in states other than the states of Assam, Meghalaya, Tripura, and Mizoram. The administration of tribes of these states is undertaken under the provisions of the Sixth Schedule.

Under the provisions of the Fifth Schedule, the executive power of a state extends to the scheduled areas therein. In the state having Scheduled Tribes, a Tribes Advisory Council is established which consists of not more than twenty members, of whom about three-fourths are the representatives of Scheduled Tribes in the Legislative Assembly of the state. The Council advises on matters pertaining to the welfare and advancement of the Scheduled Tribes as may be referred by the Governor. The Governor may direct that any particular Act of Parliament or of the State Legislature cannot apply to the Scheduled Area or can be applied with exception and modifications. The Governor may also make regulations for the peace and good governance of any Scheduled Area.

As per the provisions of the Sixth Schedule, the tribal areas in the states of Assam, Meghalaya, Tripura and Mizoram are an autonomous district. If there are different Scheduled Tribes in an autonomous district, the Governor may divide the area inhabited by them into autonomous regions.

District and Regional Councils

As per the Constitution, every autonomous district has a District Council. It consists of not more than thirty members, of whom not more than four persons are nominated by the Governor and the remainders are elected on the basis of adult franchise. A separate Regional Council is constituted for each autonomous region in the district. Both these Councils are bodies corporate and have perpetual succession and a common seal and can sue and be sued against. The administration of the area vests in these councils.

The elected members of the District Council hold office for a term of five years from the date appointed for the first meeting of the council. The term may be extended by the Governor for a period not exceeding one year at a time and in any case where a proclamation of Emergency is in operation, not beyond a period of six months after the proclamation has ceased to operate.

These councils have power to make laws with respect to the allotment, occupation or use of land other than which is a reserved forest for the purposes of agriculture or grazing or for residential or any other purpose likely to promote the interests of the inhabitants of any village or town; the management of any forest not being reserved forest; the use of any canal or water course for the purpose of agriculture; the regulation of the practice of 'jhum' or other forms of shifting cultivation; the establishment of village or town committees or councils and their powers; any other matter relating to village and town administration including police, public health and sanitation; the appointment or succession of chief or headman; the inheritance of property; marriage and divorce and social customs. All the laws are submitted to the Governor and until assented to by him, have no effect. The councils may constitute village councils or courts for the trial of suits and cases between the parties all of whom belong to Scheduled Tribes. The councils exercise the powers of a court of appeal in respect of all suits and cases triable by village council or court. The District Council may establish, construct or manage primary schools, dispensaries, markets, cattle ponds, ferries, roads, road transport and waterways in the district. These councils have the powers to assess and collect revenue in respect of such lands in accordance with the principles being followed by the government of the state in assessing lands for the purpose of land revenue in the State generally. They have power to levy and collect taxes on lands and buildings, and tolls on persons residing therein. The District Council has power to levy and collect all or any of the taxes on professions, trades, callings and employments, on animals, vehicles and boats, on the entry of goods into a market for sale and tolls on passengers and goods carried in ferries as also taxes for the maintenance of schools, dispensaries or roads.

After more than fifty years of Independence it is of immense interest to study whether the North-Eastern region, experiencing steady urban growth, is diversifying. The recent Constitutional Amendments have created a new era for local administration. Consequently, the Government of India constituted a Committee of the Members of Parliament (1995) to study and suggest whether the new enactments can be made applicable to the Scheduled Areas as well.

The committee suggested that "the urban centres in the Scheduled Areas may be grouped in three categories, viz.

(i) transitional areas comprising small trading/ administrative social service centres with mixed urban and rural or *quasba* character. These centres could be designated as Nagar Panchayats;

(ii) the larger urban centres functioning as administrative and trading centres with higher level of social services. These centres may be known as Municipal Council. Some of the municipal councils in course of time may graduate to the status of municipal corporations; and

(iii) industrial and mining townships which have a special character with potential for separate category".

The committee made further recommendations that "Nagar Panchayats should perform all functions of the Gram Panchayats. They should have a standing committee for rural development to cater to the conventional functions of the Gram Panchayats. With regards to the composition of Nagar Panchayats, not less than a half of the members should be from the Scheduled Tribes. The Intermediate Panchayat should have an Urban Affairs Committee for guiding the affairs of Nagar Panchayats within its jurisdiction in accordance with the objectives set for them in law. The Autonomous District Council should also have an Urban Affairs Committee which may guide the functioning of the Urban Affairs Committees of the Intermediate Panchayats and help the Nagar Panchayats develop in harmony with the tribal economy and their development."

In the case of each industrial and mining township, the committee suggested that "the zone of its influence should be identified and a comprehensive plan prepared for its development by a special body comprising of representatives of the municipality, the industrial and mining projects, the local administration and the Panchayats under which the area falls. This task should be completed within a period of two years".

In view of the recommendations of the Committee of the Members of Parliament and also in the light of the urban growth and growing demand of urban infrastructure and services and more so, consequent upon the Constitutional provisions, it becomes necessary to make a study of the region: its demographic characteristics, cultural heritage, special constitutional status, pattern of urbanization, local administration, municipal laws, etc., before taking any concrete decision in respect of municipal administration.

URBAN SCENARIO

Arunachal Pradesh

Arunachal Pradesh or the land of the rising sun, was earlier known as the North-East Frontier Agency (NEFA), was administered by the Ministry of External Affairs with the Governor of Assam acting as an agent of the President. It evolved as a Union Territory on 20 January, 1972. Ultimately, Arunachal Pradesh attained statehood on 20 February, 1987 (Mitra). The history of Arunachal Pradesh can be traced to only when Ahom kings began to rule Assam in the 16th century. The British took possession of Assam in 1838 and brought Arunachal Pradesh also under their administrative control. Post Independence, it was a part of North-East Frontier Agency, and later, made a Union Territory.

Area wise it is the largest state in the North-East region. It consists of the submontane and mountainous ranges sloping to the plains of Assam. The mountainous terrain of the state is composed of a variety of tribes. Barring only 12 towns, the entire area is rural where an overwhelming 88 per cent of its population lives. Agriculture is the mainstay of the people. About four per cent of the total geographical area was brought under agriculture till August 1987, while forests covered about 62 per cent of the area. Endowed with abundant forest, mineral and hydel power resources, Arunachal Pradesh has a high industrial potential.

The first full-fledged census operation in Arunachal Pradesh was held in 1961. During the census of 1961, the whole of the state was declared as rural. It was from 1971 that the process of urbanization took shape in this state. In 1971 the State had 3.70 per cent of total population in urban areas. It rose to 6.56 per cent in 1981 and further to 12.21 per cent in 1991. The rapid growth of urban population in Arunachal Pradesh is attributable to the establishment and expansion of administrative centres in the state (Bhattacharjee). The decadal rate of urban growth of Arunachal Pradesh was 139.63 per cent during 1971-81 and 152.98 per cent during 1981-91. The number of towns in Arunachal Pradesh was four in 1971 and six in 1981, which rose to ten in 1981-91. An important feature of the growth of urban settlements in Arunachal Pradesh is the dominant role of intra-state migration rather than inter-state rural-urban migration. In 1971 the state had only five districts, and the number rose to nine in 1981 and 11 in 1991.

The basic constraint of the development of urban centres in Arunachal Pradesh is the communication bottlenecks. In this state, the approach roads to all the towns are routed through the roads of Assam. There is no link road connecting the towns of Arunachal Pradesh within the state which is detrimental for the marketing of the produce of the state. Consequently, the produce is localised and there is no scope for the growth of wholesale market in the state. Besides, the geographical condition of the state is also an impediment to the growth of towns.

Arunachal Pradesh is the largest tribal state in the region but has no area under the Fifth or Sixth Schedules. The only special provision for the state under Art 371H concerns the special responsibility and powers of the governor with respect to law and order in the state and the issue of self-governance and extension of other laws in the state. Accordingly, Arunachal Pradesh does not find a mention in Art 243ZC. Therefore Part IX-A of the Constitution automatically covers Arunachal Pradesh without any modification. Despite having more than one-tenth urban population, the State has no urban local government as enunciated in the Constitution and no municipal laws have been enacted.

Assam

The political map of Assam has undergone several changes during the past decades. As a result, Assam, today is a reduced region. It is remarkable that the people of Assam have reconciled to the Union Government's bid to bring about integration in this region by fragmenting the State into separate units.

Scholars are not in consensus on the origin of the name 'Assam'. Some opine that Assam is called so because of its uneven terrain. They rely on a similar sounding Sanskrit word 'Asoma' meaning peerless. The land whose bewitching picture is conjured up by the name 'Asam' is in fact peerless, judging by the exquisite natural beauty, cultural richness and human wealth endowed to it. Geographically, Assam is now a shadow of its former self. It has been reduced to one-third of its original size in the past few decades. In 1947, Assam had an area of over 2 lakh sq. kms. excluding the then North East Frontier Agency, and current Arunachal Pradesh. Today, the current area of Assam is only 78,523 sq. kms. comprising 23 districts. The state covers about 2.39 per cent of the total area of the country.

During the epic period Assam was known as 'Pragjyothis' and later as 'Kamrupa'. Guwahati, the pulsating capital of Assam, is an ancient town whose history dates back to the Puranic days.

Assam is situated in the north-east corner of India and is bounded by Bhutan and Arunachal Pradesh on the north, Nagaland and Manipur on the east, Meghalaya and Mizoram on the south and Bangladesh, Tripura and West Bengal on the west. Only a narrow strip of submountane region of the Himalayas connects Assam with the Indian mainland. Assam is dominated by the Brahmaputra river whose total length from the source to the sea is 29 kms. and has 120 tributaries. Rainfall in Assam is one of the highest in the world.

As it is today, Assam may be divided into two important physical regions — the Barak Valley, and the Brahmaputra Valley. Agriculture covers slightly less than two-thirds of labour force. Of agriculture-based industries, tea occupies an important place. A good share of the economy of the State has increasingly been contributed by the tea industry. Assam has an exclusive range of colourful festivals. There are also a larger number of places of tourist interest.

Assam is mainly based on an agricultural economy. Agriculture plays a vital role in the development of social strata, but is alone not the only contributory factor to the development of townships. The most important factor is industrialization of the state and Assam is still industrially backward. The tea industry is the only big industry that falls under agricultural sector. Second, the development of trade, commerce, liberal professions and opportunities of higher education are some other factors which attract the rural people to settle in the urban areas. However, most of the urban centres in Assam are so contiguous to the villages, that it becomes difficult to demarcate the actual town area from that of the village area. There is no denying the fact that a significant percentage of urban population in Assam comprises outsiders from various states of India. The indigenous people are less willing to migrate to the urban centres unless they are assured of good employment opportunities and other business avocations to earn their livelihood (Bhuyan).

Assam is the largest state in the region. About eleven per cent of its population inhabits in 91 urban centres. The state has been experiencing higher decennial growth. The four class one towns account for more than one-third of its total urban population. Assam has all the three types of urban local bodies. The Assam Municipal Act, 1956 regulates the functioning of Nagar Panchayat or Town Committee and Municipal Board, while the lone Municipal Corporation of Guwahati has its separate Act.

Manipur

Manipur, which is characterized by its economic backwardness is a small state having a total geographical area of only 22,327 sq. kms. of which 90 per cent is covered by hills. The physiographical feature of the state, therefore, presents notably two distinct areas, viz., the valley and the hilly area, which are conspicuous by their absence of uniform development strategies for the past many decades whereby the valley has been placed in a favourable position with higher concentration of population of about 70 per cent of the total population of the state (Singh).

In terms of the annual rate of growth of urbanization in Manipur, especially during 1951-81, it registered an increase of

37.22 per cent during the decade 1951-61. This declined to 7.65 per cent during 1961-71 as against 10.25 per cent during 1971-81. Therefore it was with the increase in the level of urbanization, measured in terms of the percentage of urban population to the total population of the state over the year 1951-81, that the population living in urban area has multiplied about 134times during the same period. An important characteristic is that about 87.97 per cent of the total urban population of the state is still in the valley area. In other words, the process of urbanization in Manipur is, by and large, a process of urban agglomeration mainly in the valley area unaccompanied by industrialization and expansion of necessary urban amenities leaving the hill area still predominantly rural (Singh).

The hill areas of Manipur for which District Councils exist, have been excluded from the purview of Part IX; however, there is no such exemption vide Art 243ZC in relation to municipalities. Moreover, confusion is likely to be created when Part IX has been extended to the valley and Part IXA to the entire state with the hill areas left without any guidelines.

The State has more than one fourth of its population inhabiting in 30 towns, comprising lone class-one town accounting about 40 per cent of total urban population. The state has the Manipur Municipalities Act, 1994 providing administrative provisions for all the three types of urban local bodies, although there is no municipal corporation in the State.

Meghalaya

Meghalaya, literally meaning the abode of clouds, is essentially a hilly state. Meghalaya was created as an autonomous State within the State of Assam on 2nd April, 1970. The full-fledged State of Meghalaya came into existence on 21st January, 1972. It is bounded on the north and east by Assam and on the south and west by Bangladesh. Meghalaya is divided into seven administrative districts. These are predominantly inhabited by the Khasis, the Jaintias and the Garos. These tribal communities are the descendants of very ancient people having distinctive traits and ethnic origin.

Meghalaya is basically an agricultural state. Eightythree per cent of the total population depends primarily on agriculture for livelihood. The topography, physical features and land conditions as prevailing in the State provide extremely limited scope for extensive cultivation or to bring additional area under net cultivation.

The total forest area in the State is 9357 sq. kms., with only 993 sq. km. under the control of the State Government and the rest under the District Councils and private managements. Meghalaya is also rich in wildlife. The state has two national parks and two wildlife sanctuaries.

The state has seven towns (1991) containing about 19 per cent of its population. Surprisingly, it has been witnessing the lowest decadal urban growth in the region. Though the level of urbanization in Meghalaya is low, the growth rate of urban population in the state had been very high which has been putting pressure on the existing civic amenities.

Meghalaya has a unique system of urban administration. It consists of many other components concerning the District Council and the traditional leadership. The District Council acts as the executive and legislative authority in respect of specific matters mentioned in the Sixth Schedule of the Constitution. The Council mainly has powers with regard to: (i) the allotment, occupation, use or the setting a part of land for the purpose of agriculture or grazing or for residential or other non-agricultural purposes or for any other purpose likely to promote the interests of the inhabitants of any village or town; (ii) the management of any forest not being reserved forest; (iii) the use of any canal or water course for the purpose of agriculture; (iv) the regulation of the practice of jhum or other forms of shifting cultivation; (v) the establishment of village or town committees or councils and their powers; (vi) any other matter relating to village and town police and public health and sanitation; (vii) the inheritance of property; (viii) marriage and divorce; (ix) social customs; and (x) the appointment or succession of chiefs or headmen.

The District Council appoints the 'Syiem', the 'Dollois' or the 'Nokmas'. These officers are normally elected by an electoral college consisting of the entire population within the area. Both the District Council and traditional leaders take up schemes within their respective jurisdiction relating to creation and management of civic infrastructure. There are several departments of the government responsible for matters relating to urban development in the state.

Urban local administration in the State is organized by municipal boards at Shillong and Tura, a cantonment board and four town committees. The government has decided to create a municipal corporation for Shillong master plan area and a town committee at each of the subdivisional headquarters.

Presently, local bodies in the state can be created in urban areas both under the Assam Municipal Act, 1956 adopted by the Meghalaya and the relevant Act of the concerned District Councils. The Municipal Boards of Shillong and Tura have been constituted under the Assam Municipal Act, 1956, while the town committee at Jawai, Nongstoin, Williamnagar and Baghmara have been created by the District Councils. In some cases, the area of the town committee is so big that it is physically impossible for the town committee to look after civic amenities. The main sources of revenue are taxes on house, latrine, water supply, animals, market fee, service charges on government buildings, taxes on entry of vehicles, car parking, rent on land and houses, stall and shops, etc. The municipal boards are handicapped by a weak resource base and inadequate technical manpower. Both the Boards are being managed by officers for a long time (Agnihotri).

The entire territory of Meghalaya is divided into three Autonomous District Councils. The responsibility for extending both Part IX and Part IX-A rests only with the Parliament.

Mizoram

Mizoram was one of the districts of Assam till 1972 when it became Union Territory. After being annexed by the British in 1891, a part remained under Assam while the southern half remained under Bengal. Both these parts were amalgamated into one district under the Chief Commissioner of Assam. With the implementation of the North Eastern Reorganization Act, 1972, Mizoram became a Union Territory. As a sequel to the signing of the historic memorandum of settlement between the Government of India and the Mizo National Front in 1986, it was granted statehood on 20th February, 1987. It occupies an area of great strategic importance in north-eastern portion of India. Mizoram has great natural beauty and an endless variety of landscape and is rich in fauna and flora. Most of the Mizos are Christians. Mizo language has no script of its own. The missionaries introduced the Roman script for Mizo language and for formal education. About 60 per cent of the people of Mizoram are engaged in agricultural pursuits. The entire state of Mizoram is a Notified Backward Area and is categorized under No Industry District. However, concerted efforts are being made to accelerate the growth of industries in the State.

The proportion of urban population in Mizoram has increased considerably from 3.54 per cent in 1951 to 5.36 per cent in 1961, 11.14 per cent in 1971, 24.67 per cent in 1981 and 46.20 per cent in 1991. The decadal growth of urban population has been recorded as 105.14 per cent during 1951-61, 164.85 per cent during 1961-71, 222.61 per cent during 1971-81 and 160.27 per cent during 1981-91. The fall in the recent decennial growth rate of urban population as compared to the increasing trend in the previous three decades is mainly due to sharp fall in the growth rate of the two larger towns of Mizoram, namely Aizawal and Lunglei which together constitute about 59 per cent of the total population of urban Mizoram (Agarwal).

The state enjoys the distinction of having the highest percentage (46.20) of urban population in the region. Such a huge population inhabits in 22 towns consisting of the lone class-one town covering about half (48.7 per cent) of the total urban population of the State.

In Mizoram, there are only three small Autonomous District Councils under the Sixth Schedule. The bulk of Mizo territory is not covered by it. Moreover, while the entire Mizoram and the Sixth Schedule area therein enjoy double exemption under Art 243M, only the Sixth Schedule area is exempt under Art 243ZC.

Nagaland

The Nagas are basically tribal people and every tribe has its own effective system of self-governance from time immemorial. In the 19th century the British appeared on the scene and ultimately the area was brought under British administration. After Independence, the territory was made a Centrally administered area in 1957, administered by the Governor of Assam. It was known as the Naga Hills of Tuensang Area. This failed to quell popular aspirations and unrest began. Hence, in 1961 this was renamed as Nagaland and given the status of State in the Indian Union which was formally inaugurated on 1st December, 1963. Agriculture is the main occupation of 90 per cent of the population in the State. The process of industrialization in the State is in its infancy but the need to have more industries have been well recognized. The growth of urbanization in Nagaland has been quite fast and it is even faster than in some other states of North-East India. Kohima is the capital of the State and been growing fast on account of expanding administrative and political activities. Dimapur, on the other hand, has been expanding fast due to the development of business, industries and civic and educational facilities. Each of these towns is unique in respect of its growth pattern, but both are cosmopolitan in character. These urban areas have emerged as ethnically integrated cultural centres. People who have come from outside are living together with the indigenous urbanites by integrating themselves with the latter socially, culturally and economically (Saikia).

The State has 17.28 per cent of its population centred in nine towns, comprising two class-two towns inhabiting more than half of its urban population. The decadal growth has been remarkable. No part of Nagaland is scheduled. However, there is a special provision for the state in the Constitution (Art 371A). The State has been exempted from coverage by Part IX but not from Part IXA.

Tripura

Tripura is the second smallest state in the country. It is strategically situated between the river valleys of Myanmar and Bangladesh. It is surrounded by Bangladesh on all sides, except for a narrow sector in the north-east, where it borders on Assam and Mizoram. Tripura was a Hindu state of great antiquity having been ruled by the Maharajas for 1300 years before its accession to the Indian Union.

The History of Tripura dates back to the *Mahabharata*, the *Puranas* and pillar inscriptions of emperor Ashoka. There are no historical records available of Tripura except *Rajmala* which is the chronicle of the Kings of the ruling family of Tripura. Nineteenth century marked the beginning of the modern era in Tripura when king Maharaja Berchandra Manikya Bahadur modelled his administrative set-up on the British Indian pattern and brought in various reforms. His successors ruled Tripura till 15th October, 1945, when it was annexed to the Indian Union. After Independence, it became a part 'C' State and with the reorganization of states in 1956, it became a Centrally administered territory. On 21st January, 1972, this territory attained the status of a full-fledged state.

The state covers an area of 10,491 sq. kms., about 0.32 per cent of the total area of the country is divided in three districts. Tea production is the major industry in Tripura. The sericulture industry in the state is also developing fast.

About 15 per cent of the State's population lives in 18 towns comprising lone class-one town having more than one-third (37.6 per cent) of its urban people inhabiting therein.

Urbanization in Tripura has taken place with Agartala as the nucleus. Agartala's overwhelming preeminence as an urban centre in Tripura originates from the fact that it has been the capital of Tripura and urbanization of this industrially backward state has been caused mainly by the expansion of the administrative infrastructure (Bhattacharjee). As the flow of migrants from Bangladesh slowed down after 1961, the decadal rate of growth of urban population fell from 141.80 per cent during 1951-61 to 57.63 per cent during 1961-71. But even during 1961-71, the rate of growth of total population of Tripura and consequently, proportion of urban population went on increasing although at a slow pace. During 1961-71, increase in urban population was mainly the result of the increase in the density of population of the existing towns as no new towns came to be recognized and the areas of the towns also did not register any notable increase. The rate of urban growth registered a further fall in the decade of 1971-81. This happened in spite of the fact that four new towns, viz., Amarpur, Sonamura, Kamalpur and Sabroom came into existence during this period. It is also found that during 1971-81, the rate of growth of urban population of Tripura only marginally exceeded that of total population of the state and consequently there was very little change in the proportion of urban population during this decade. The 1981-91 decade witnessed a very appreciable (87.75 per cent) increase in urban population of Tripura and subsequently, the proportion of urban population which was in the neighbourhood of 10 per cent in 1971 and 1981, reached 15.26 per cent in 1991.

In Tripura, although the tribal area is neither comparatively small nor compact, has been brought under the ambit of the Sixth Schedule and an Autonomous District Council has been constituted. It is for Parliament to make a law for extending the provisions of Parts IX and IXA to the Scheduled Areas in Tripura.

There is the Tripura Municipal Act, 1994 to administer all the three types of urban local bodies, i.e., nagar panchayat, municipal council and municipal corporation (the last mentioned is not in existence).

Sikkim

The early history of Sikkim starts in the 13th century with the signing of a brotherhood treaty between the Lipcha chieftain and the Tibetan prince. The Namgyal dynasty began rule since 1642. Sikkim formally became an integral part of the Indian Union in 1975.

Sikkim lies in the heart of the towering Himalayas. It is bounded by Nepal in the west, Bhutan in the south-east, Tibet in the north and north-east and West Bengal in the south. Most of the area of the state consists of ravines and green valleys. The third highest mountain peak in the world, Kanchenjunga is situated on Sikkim's western border. Its dense forests are ideal habitat for wildlife.

State's economy is basically agrarian. It has the largest area under cultivation and highest production of cardamom in India. The state has been declared as industrially backward. Road length in the state is 2383 kms. Two closest railway stations are Siliguri (114 kms) and New Jalpaiguri (125 kms.). There is no airport in Sikkim.

The state's population is comprised of the three principal ethnic communities of the Bhutias, the Lepchas and Nepalese.

Sikkim witnessed a tremendous increase in its urban population during the 1971-81 decade. The following decade (1981-91), however, recorded a decline in urban population. There was only one town in Sikkim, in 1951. In 1961, the number rose to 6 and to 8, in 1981. Surprisingly, there are no class one and two towns in Sikkim. The majority of towns fall under class three category. The urban local bodies are in the process of being constituted. The State has enacted the Sikkim Municipalities Act, 1995 for its urban governance.

ANNEXURE 1
PERCENTAGE OF URBAN POPULATION AND DECADAL GROWTH (1971-81) IN THE NORTH-EASTERN STATES

	%age of Urban Population			*Decadal Growth*	
	1971	*1981*	*1991*	*1971-81*	*1981-91*
Arunachal Pradesh	3.70	6.65	12.21	139.63	152.98
Assam	8.81	*	11.80	-	91.66
Manipur	13.19	26.42	27.69	165.36	34.73
Meghalaya	14.55	18.07	18.69	63.98	36.36
Mizoram	11.36	24.67	46.20	222.61	160.27
Nagaland	9.95	15.52	17.28	133.95	74.74
Tripura	10.43	10.99	15.26	38.93	85.75
Sikkim	-	16.15	9.12	159.73	(-)27.60

* No census was held in 1981.

ANNEXURE 2
NUMBER OF CLASS I AND II TOWNS (1971-81) IN THE NORTH-EASTERN STATES

	1971			1981			1991		
	Total	Class I	Class II	Total	Class I	Class II	Total	Class I	Class II
Arunachal Pradesh	4	-	-	6	-	-	10	-	-
Assam*	69	1 (15.5)	5 (24.4)	-	-	-	87	4 (37.6)	4 (11.7)
Manipur	8	1 (70.9)	-	32	1 (41.7)	-	30	1 (39.7)	-
Meghalaya	3	1 (83.4)	-	7	1 (72.4)	-	7	1 (48.7)	-
Mizoram	2	-	-	6	-	1 (61.2)	22	1 (48.7)	-
Nagaland	3	-	-	7	-	-	9	-	2 (52.4)
Tripura	6	1 (61.8)	-	10	1 (58.6)	-	18	1 (37.6)	-
Sikkim	7	-	-	8	-	-	8	-	-

* No census was held in 1981
Figures in parenthesis denote percentage of population.

ANNEXURE 3
POPULATION STATISTICS IN THE NORTH-EASTERN STATES DURING 1981 AND 1991

	Density		Population (1981) (%)		Literacy (1991) (%)	
	1981	1991	SC	ST	Total	Urban
Arunachal Pradesh	8	10	0.5	69.8	41.59	71.59
Assam	230	286	-	-	52.89	79.39
Manipur	64	82	1.3	27.3	59.89	70.53
Meghalaya	60	79	0.4	80.6	49.10	81.74
Mizoram	23	33	Negligible	93.6	82.27	93.95
Nagaland	47	73	-	84.0	61.65	83.10
Tripura	196	263	15.1	28.4	60.44	83.09
Sikkim	45	57	-	-	47.0	70.15

REFERENCES

1. Agarwal, A.K., A Study in Urbanisation in Pattern in Mizoram, *Ibid*: 265-270.
2. Bhattacharjee, P.R., Urbanisation of Tripura: Pattern and Problem *Ibid*: 283-298.
3. Bhattacharjee, R.P., Urbanisation Trend in Arunachal Pradesh: A Brief Analysis, *Ibid*: 117-125.
4. Bhuyan, P.L., and Das, N.C., The Trend of Urban Development in NER with special Reference to Assam, *Ibid*: 177-187.
5. Butola, B.S., Urbanisation and Underdevelopment in the North Eastern India, *Ibid*: 39-48.
6. *Census of India*, 1971, 1981, 1991.
7. *India Year Book*, 1994, 1995, 1996.
8. John, P.H., Urbanisation in North East India: A Trend, Ibid, 48-53.
9. Maheshwari, S.R., The North Eastern Region (The Politics of Late coming). In Iqbal Narain (ed.), *State Politics in India*, Delhi: Meenakshi, 1976: 463-476.
10. Mitra, A., The Trends and Pattern of Urbanisation in Arunachal Pradesh, 1971-81: A District-wise Study, *Ibid*: 126-134.
11. Nayak, D.K., Chakraborty, S and Chakravarty, S., Pattern of Urbanisation in the North-East, p. 1-14 in J.B. Ganguly (ed) *Urbanization and Development in North East India (Trends, and Policy Implication)*, Deep & Deep, New Delhi, 1995.
12. Report of the Committee of the Members of Parliament (1995), Government of India, New Delhi.
13. Saikia J.K.K., Process of Urbanisation in Nagaland: A Case Study of Kohima and Dimapur Towns, *Ibid*: 271-282.
14. Sharma, M.L., The Troubled North East, in *Ibid*: 437-462.
15. Sharma, H.N., and Kar, B.K., Pattern of Population Growth in North East India. In A. Ahmad, D. Noin and H.N. Sharma (eds.), *Demographic Transition (The Third World Scenario)*, Rawat Publications, 1997, 73-94.
16. Singh, L.T., Urbanisation in Manipur: An Analysis in Retrospect, *Ibid*: 206-276.
17. *The Imperial Gazetteer of India*, Vol. IV, Oxford, 1909.

TWO

Assam

In Assam all the three types of urban local bodies exist. There is only one Municipal Corporation Guwahati, the capital city which has a separate Act, i.e., the Guwahati Municipal Corporation Act, 1969. The other two types, i.e., Nagar Panchayats or Town Committees and the Municipal Boards are governed by the Assam Municipal Act, 1956.

NAGAR PANCHAYAT OR TOWN COMMITTEE

The State Government by notification declares the specified transitional area, a notified area, to be termed as 'Small Town'. For each of such notified areas a Town Committee is formed. It consists of such number of members as may be fixed by the State Government from time to time. In notified areas the State Government may impose any tax which could have been imposed therein, if such areas were a municipality; apply or adopt for the assessment and recovery of any tax; arrange for the due expenditure of the proceeds of taxes and of other funds; and extend provisions of the Municipal Act subject to certain restrictions and modifications as the State Government may think fit.

Constitution of Municipal Board

Each municipality has a body of commissioners designated as Municipal Board. It consists of :

(i) Elected Commissioners: Not less than ten but not more than

(ii) Appointed Members : The State Government may appoint persons having special knowledge or experience in Municipal Administration;

(iii) Ex-Officio Members : a) MPs and MLAs,
b) Chairman of Wards Committee.

The Appointed Members have the right to attend and speak at all meetings but do not have the right to vote.

Reservation

In every municipality seats are reserved:

(i) for the Scheduled Castes and Scheduled Tribes in proportion of their population to the total population;
(ii) one-third of the seats to the women belonging to the Scheduled Castes and Scheduled Tribes;
(iii) one-third of seats for the women.

Eligibility for Election

A person is not eligible for election as Commissioner if such person is not entitled to vote at the election of Commissioners, or has been adjudged by a competent court to be of unsound mind or an uncertified bankrupt or an undischarged insolvent or has, during the four years immediately preceding the election, been convicted of an offence or imprisonment for an offence involving moral turpitude or served any portion of a sentence or has been ordered by court to furnish security for good behaviour or has been declared by notification to be disqualified for employment in the public service or during the four years immediately preceding the election been debarred from practising as a legal practitioner or is a salaried servant of Government or is an employee of any Local Authority or is in arrear for more than three months, on the date of submission of nomination paper, of any dues to the municipality, or he is so disqualified for the purposes of elections to the State Legislature.

Resignation And Removal of Commissioners

A Commissioner may resign by writing under his hand addressed to the Chairman and thereupon he is deemed to have vacated the office. The Chairman forthwith informs the Deputy

Commissioner or the Sub Divisional Officer of the resignation and also informs the next meeting of the Municipal Board or Town Committee.

The State Government may remove any elected Commissioner on the following grounds: on the ground of misconduct in the discharge of his duties, if removal is recommended by a resolution of the Board passed at a special meeting and supported by votes of not less than two-thirds of the whole number of Commissioners OR if he ceases to reside within the municipality continuously for a period of twelve months OR if he refuses to act or becomes incapable of acting as a Commissioner Or if he has been declared by the State Government by notification to have violated his oath or affirmation to allegiance OR if without an excuse, sufficient in the opinion of the State Government, he absents himself from four consecutive meetings of the Board OR if, being a legal practitioner, he appears against the Board before any court in his professional capacity in any case instituted by or against the Board OR if the becomes disabled in view of other qualifications OR if he knowingly acquires or continues to hold without the permission in writing of the State Government, directly or indirectly, or by a partner, any share or interest in any contract, or employment with, by or on behalf of the Board OR if he is in arrears of any kind of dues to the municipality after a bill or a notice has been duly served upon him. The State Government may, after consultation with the Board remove any Commissioner if his continuance is dangerous to the public peace or order or likely to bring the administration of Board into contempt. However, no Commissioner can be removed unless he has been given an opportunity of showing cause against the order of removal. Such a removed person is not eligible for election or re-election without the consent of the State Government.

Disqualification of Commissioners

A Commissioner becomes disqualified to continue in office if he, without the written permission of the State Government, Directly or indirectly, has any share or interest in any contract, lease, sale or purchase of land or any agreement, or holds office of profit under it.

A Commissioner cannot vote on any matter affecting his own conduct or pecuniary interest or on any question which regards exclusively the assessment of himself or the valuation of any property in respect of which he is directly or indirectly interested or of any property of or for which he is a manager or agent for his liability to any tax.

Chairman and Vice-Chairman

At the first meeting of the Board, called at the instance of the Deputy Commissioner or the Sub-Divisional Officer, the Commissioners elect one from amongst themselves for the post of Chairman. The election is subject to the approval of the State Government. The Commissioners at the same meeting or at a subsequent meeting, elect one of them as Vice-Chairman.

The first meeting is held on the date fixed by the Deputy Commissioner or the Sub Divisional Officer. Whenever he considers necessary, he may vary the date. The date fixed for the meeting is notified in the Official Gazette, at least 15 clear days before the meeting. The Deputy Commissioner or the Sub Divisional Officer sends copies of the notification fixing the date to the members at least seven days before meeting is held. The Magistrate appoints a member of the Board to preside at the meeting. The President first makes the oath or affirmation himself and then administers the oath to the other members present whether there is quorum or not. In case of quorum the meeting proceeds to elect or requests the State Government to appoint a Chairman. If the quorum is not present or if the first meeting proves infructuous, the meeting stands adjourned to some future date to be appointed by the Magistrate, who causes at least three days notice of the adjourned meeting to be given to the members. The members present at the adjourned meeting form a quorum whatever may be their number and be competent to elect a Chairman.

Any member may nominate any member before the noon of the day preceding the date fixed for the meeting. The President reads out to the Board the names of the members who have been duly nominated together with those of their proposers and seconders. The election is held by ballot. Where more than two candidates have been nominated and at the first ballot no candidate obtains more votes than the aggregate votes obtained by the other candidates, the candidate who has obtained the smallest number of votes is excluded and balloting is proceeded until one candidate obtains more votes than the remaining candidate or, than the aggregate votes of the remaining candidates. Where at any ballot, any of three or more candidates obtain equal votes and one of them has to be excluded, the determination of the candidate to be excluded is made by drawing of lots.

If the Commissioners fail to elect a Chairman or a Vice-Chairman,the State Government appoints by name one of the Commissioners to be Chairman or Vice Chairman or directs the Deputy Commissioner or the Sub-Divisional Officer to fix another date for the purpose of elections. In that case, the Government may appoint a government Official to be Chairman or Vice-Chairman.

Whenever the offices of both the Chairman and the Vice-Chairman are vacant in any Board, the State Government can appoint any one from amongst the Commissioners, as the Chairman to hold office, as such temporarily, till a Chairman is elected.

Every Chairman and every Vice-Chairman holds office from the date of his election to the date of election of the Chairman after the next general election.

The Board at a meeting, may grant leave of absence to its Chairman or Vice-Chairman, for a period not exceeding three months in any one year. If a Chairman or Vice-Chairman overstays his leave beyond three months, he is deemed to have vacated his office and the acting person continues to act for him till the vacancy is filled up by a fresh election at the next meeting of the Board.

For filling of casual vacancy in the office of the Chairman and Vice-Chairman, in case of vacancy in the office of the Chairman, the Vice-Chairman, and in the case of vacancy in the office of Vice-Chairman, the Chairman can call a meeting to complete the election within 45 days of the occurrence of the vacancy. If the Chairman or the Vice-Chairman fails to call the meeting, the Deputy Commissioner or the Sub-Divisional Officer can call the meeting. A meeting for election of the Chairman is presided over by the Vice-Chairman, unless he is himself a candidate for election or for other reasons intimates to the Deputy Commissioner or the Sub-

Divisional Officer in writing about his inability to preside. In such an event, any Commissioner who is not a candidate for the office of the Chairman may be nominated by the Deputy Commissioner or the Sub-Divisional Officer to preside over.

Resignation and Removal of Chairman and Vice-Chairman

An elected Chairman may resign by laying notice in writing of his intention to do so before the Board at a meeting with intimation to the District Magistrate and the Commissioner of the Division. He ceases to hold office on laying such notice.

A Vice Chairman may resign by writing under his hand addressed to the Chairman and thereupon he deems to have vacated the office. The Chairman forthwith informs the Deputy Commissioner or the Sub-Divisional Officer of the resignation and also informs the next meeting of the Board or Committee.

The State Government after giving an opportunity to explain may remove the Chairman or Vice-Chairman from his office if he is persistently omitting or refusing to carry out or disobeying the provisions or lawful orders or he becomes incapable of so acting or is declared insolvent or is convicted for any offence involving moral turpitude.

Powers of Chairman

For the transaction of business the Chairman exercises all the powers vested by the Act in the Board. He may in cases of emergency direct the execution of any work or doing of any act and the immediate execution or doing of any work, which is necessary for the service or safety of the public, and may direct that the expense incurred, be paid from the municipal fund. He forthwith reports the action taken and the reasons therefor to the Board at next meeting.

The Chairman may delegate to the Vice-Chairman all or any of the duties and powers and may at any time withdraw or modify it. During the vacancy in the office of Vice-Chairman or in the absence of Vice-Chairman on leave or otherwise, the Chairman may, by an order in writing, delegate any of his functions to any Commissioner till the Vice-Chairman resumes office or a new Vice-Chairman is elected or appointed. Every such order is communicated to the Municipal Board at the next meeting.

Duties of Vice-Chairman

The Vice-Chairman performs any of the duties and exercises any of the powers of the Chairman during a vacancy in the office of the Chairman or temporary absence of the Chairman. He performs any duty and exercises any powers delegated to him.

Allowances

The Chairman and Vice-Chairman may, if Board thinks fit, receive conveyance allowances out of the municipal fund. Such allowances are subject to the approval of the State Government. The Commissioners are not paid from municipal fund any salary or remuneration but may be allowed travelling allowance when admissible.

Election Petition

The validity of an election can be questioned by an unsuccessful candidate or person qualified to vote at the election at any time within 21 days after the date of declaration of the result of election. Such an election petition is filed before the District Judge of the district within which the election has been or should have been held.

The petitioner is required to deposit one hundred rupees in Court as security for the costs. The Deputy Commissioner or the Sub-Divisional Officer may also be authorised by the State Government to receive election petition on behalf of the District Judge for transmission to him.

The District Judge or any judicial officer subordinate to him and not below the rank of Subordinate Judge may, after holding inquiry pass an order confirming or amending the declared result or setting the election aside.

An appeal lies to the District Judge from any decision or order of a Subordinate Judge. A decision or order of the District Judge is final. If the Judge sets aside an election he may declare any person by whom a corrupt practice has been committed, to be disqualified from being a candidate for election for a period not exceeding five years from the date of decision, and the Judge's decision is final.

Committees

The Board at a meeting may appoint committees to assist it in the discharge of any specific duties or class of duties devolving upon it. It may delegate to any such committee all or any of its powers, or withdraw all, or any of such powers necessary for the purpose of rendering assistance. Each committee consists of Commissioners and of residents with special qualifications appointed by the Board at its meeting. The number of Commissioners is not less than two-thirds of the whole number of members of the committee. All questions connected with the removal or resignation of Commissioners from committee are settled by the Board at a meeting. The proceedings of committee are subject to confirmation by the Board at a meeting.

Joint Committee

Any Municipal Board may join with other Local Authorities or with any cantonment authority or with more than one such authorities. A joint committee consists of not more than two Commissioners/members from each of such bodies.

Conduct of Business

The Commissioners meet for the transaction of business at their office, at least once in every month and as often as a meeting is called by the Chairman or in his absence by the Vice-Chairman. If there be no business to be laid before the Commissioners at any monthly meeting, the Chairman instead of calling the meeting gives notice of the fact to each Commissioner, three days before the date which is appointed for the monthly meeting. The Chairman or in his absence the Vice-Chairman may call a special meeting whenever he thinks fit and can call one on a requisition signed by not less than three of the Commissioners. If the Chairman or the Vice-Chairman fails to call a special meeting within twenty days after a requisition is made, the meeting may be called by the persons who signed the requisition.

The Chairman or in his absence the Vice-Chairman presides at every meeting. In the absence of both, the Commissioners choose one of them to preside. A member duly elected at the meeting presides, if the resolution relates to the simultaneous removal of both the Chairman and the Vice-Chairman.

All questions at a meeting are determined by a majority of votes of the Commissioners present. In the case of equality of votes, on any question other than the election of the Chairman or the Vice-Chairman, the President has a second vote. In the case of equality of votes in the election of Chairman, Vice-Chairman or President, the determination is made by the drawal of lots.

Minutes of the proceedings of all meetings are entered into a book and are signed by the President of the meeting. It is published in prescribed manner and is open to the inspection of the tax-payers at all reasonable times and without charge. A copy of the minutes is forthwith forwarded by the Board to the Deputy Commissioner and the Commissioner of the Division and another copy is submitted to the State Government. The minutes are laid before the next meeting for confirmation and are also signed by the President if the same are correctly entered.

Quorum

No business is transacted at any meeting unless it has been called by the Chairman or Vice-Chairman or by persons signing a requisition, nor unless a quorum is present.

In the case of disposal of subjects relating to scale of establishment and salaries, the framing of bye-laws, the annual budget estimates, the appointment or fixing of the pay or allowance of a paid Secretary, Engineer, Water Works Superintendent, Health Officer, Assessor or Executive Officer, imposition of taxes, fees and tolls, the election of Chairman or Vice-Chairman, the raising of loan, the subject of a meeting specially convened the quorum should be one-half of the total number of Commissioners. For all other business, the quorum should be one-third of the total Commissioners.

If at any meeting, the quorum is not present, the meeting is adjourned to some future day appointed by the President and three days notice is given. The Commissioners present at adjourned meeting for transaction of business other than specifically mentioned earlier, form the quorum, whatever their number may be.

Establishment

The Board determines and appoints the establishment employed by it and fixes the salaries and allowances to such establishment. The Chairman makes all appointments if the monthly salary of the office does not carry more than fifty rupees or a salary rising by periodical increments to more than fifty rupees. The Chairman may remove such persons for efficiency, negligence of duty or misconduct. The appointment of any officer whose pay is wholly or partly conducted by the State Government cannot be created or abolished without the sanction of the State Government. Every nomination to or dismissal from any such appointment is subject to confirmation by State Government.

In case of disciplinary action, every employee has the right of appeal to the Board, from the orders of the Chairman or the Vice-Chairman. In case of orders involving dismissal or removal of officers not liable to be dismissed or removed by the Chairman or Vice-Chairman, an appeal to the Local Self-Government Department may be filed.

The Board at a special meeting by a resolution supported by two-thirds of the Commissioners present, makes regulations in respect of officers and employees on its staff for fixing the amount and nature of the security to be furnished, regulating the grant of leave, leave allowances and other allowances and regulating conduct and generally laying down conditions of service.

The State Government may require the board to appoint such Health Officers, Sanitary Inspectors, other public health establishments and Water Works Superintendent as it considers necessary or to employ such officers of Government as Health Officers, Sanitary Inspectors and Water Works Superintendent.

A Board may appoint an Executive Officer with the approval of the State Government. The State, Government may, if it finds that any particular Board should have an Executive Officer and the said Board does not make such an appointment, appoint any person as such officer, in respect of that particular Board. In either case, the salary of the officer and other charges are charged on Municipal Fund unless the State Government agrees to bear the same or any portion thereof. The State Government can make rules regarding the appointment, salaries, conditions of service, powers, duties and functions of the Executive Officer and other relevant matters connected therewith and also providing that no disciplinary action can be taken against the Executive Officer, except with the approval of the State Government.

Budget

The Board has to pass the annual budget estimates for the next financial year before the end of the year. When the Board fails to pass the budget due to causes beyond its control, the Director of Municipal Administration may, on application by the Board, give such extension of time as he may deem necessary to pass the budget. The budget passed in the meeting of the Board has to be approved by the Director of Municipal Administration before 31st March of the preceding year.

Contracts

The Board may enter into and perform any contract necessary for it. Every contract made by or on behalf of the Board in respect of any sum exceeding Rs 500 is sanctioned by the Board at a meeting and be in writing and signed by at least two of the members, one of whom should be the Chairman or the Vice-Chairman and is sealed with the common seal of the Board. Unless so executed a contract is not binding on the Board.

Municipal Fund

Each Board has a Municipal Fund vested in it. The balance standing at the credit, all sums received by or on behalf of the Board, all sums received as loan raised by the Board and such sums as the State Government may sanction as grants-in-aid are placed to its credit.

The Board sets apart and applies annually out of Municipal Fund, firstly the charges of its own establishment and secondly, payment of loan and interest, thirdly, the liabilities and obligations arising from the trust legally imposed upon or accepted by the Board and fourthly, the expenses on paupers, lunatics and lepers who are inhabitants of the municipalities and are sent to public asylums. The Municipal Fund may be applied for other services and provisions within the municipality and with the sanction of the Director of Municipal Administration outside the municipality.

Without the prior sanction of the State Government the municipal fund can not be spent for contesting the case filed against the Chairman, Vice-Chairman, Commissioner or any other person in authority. All orders for payment of money from the Municipal Fund for a sum not above Rs. 5000 are signed by the Chairman or a Vice-Chairman. All other orders for larger sums are signed by both the Chairman and Vice-Chairman or by one of them and another Commissioner of the Board.

Municipal Property

All public roads including the soil, pavements, stones and other materials thereof, and all drains, bridges, trees, erection, materials, implements; all public streams, channels, water-courses, springs, tanks, reservoirs, cisterns, wells, aquaducts, conduits, tunnels, pipes, pumps and other water-works; all public sewers and drains, and all works, materials and things appertaining thereto; all sewage, rubbish and offensive matter collected by the Board from roads, latrines, sewers, cesspools and other places; all public lamps, lamp-posts and apparatus connected therewith or appertaining thereto, all public gates, markets, slaughter houses and public buildings which have been constructed or are maintained out of the Municipal Fund; and all land or other property transferred to the Board or acquired by gift, purchase or otherwise vest in the Board and be under its direction, management and control.

Municipal Taxation

The municipality may impose within limits the following taxes, fees and tolls, or any of them

(i) a tax on holdings assessed on their annual value, payable by the owners;

(ii) a water tax payable by the owner or occupier on the annual value of buildings;

(iii) a lighting tax, payable by the owner or occupier, on the annual value of holdings;

(iv) a latrine tax, payable by the owner or occupier, on the annual value of holdings;

(v) a drainage tax, payable by the owner, where a system of drainage has been introduced;

(vi) a tax on private markets payable by the owner;
(vii) licence fee on carts, carriages and animals used for riding or burden;
(viii) a fee on the registration of dogs and cattle;
(ix) a fee on boats moored within the municipality;
(x) tolls on bridges;
(xi) a betterment fee on holding in any area of which value has been increased due to improvement schemes completed at Board's cost;
(xii) fees for setting up and maintenance of fire brigade;
(xiii) fees for conducting, at the cost of the Board, any scheme of social service for the improvement of public health;
(xiv) license fee on boats;
(xv) with the sanction of the State Government any other tax, tolls, rate or fee.

The taxes on holdings and private markets cannot be imposed in respect of the same premises. All municipal taxes in respect of Government holdings are payable by the Government themselves and not by occupiers. A rebate of not less than Rupees fifty per annum of the latrine tax on a holding is allowed if the holding is provided with sanitary type latrines and does not contain any service latrine.

Annual Value

The assessor after making necessary enquiries determines the valuation of all holdings and enters the same in the valuation list. For preparing the list, the assessor by notice requires the owners/occupiers of all holdings to furnish him within fifteen days, with returns of the rent of annual value and a description of the holdings. The assessor at any time between sunrise and sunset may enter, inspect and measure any holding. Whoever refuses or fails to furnish return or knowingly furnishes a false or incorrect return or description is liable to a fine not exceeding twenty rupees and to further fine not exceeding five rupees for each day during which he omits to furnish a true and correct return. A person obstructing, hindering or preventing the assessor appointed by the Board from entering or inspecting or measuring any holdings is liable to a fine not exceeding Rs. 200.

In the case of a holding with a building used or occupied for the residence by the owner himself, the annual value is lessened by 25 per cent. In case of Government buildings the annual value is deemed to be an amount which may be equal to but not exceeding six per cent of the cost of erection of the building, in addition to a reasonable ground rent of the land comprised in the holding.

A person dissatisfied with the amount assessed upon him or with the valuation or assessment, may apply to the Board to review the amount of assessment of valuation or to exempt him from the assessment of tax. Every such application is heard and determined by a committee of not more than five members or by an officer not below such rank as the State Government determines. Services of such an officer is obtained by the Board and to whom the Board at a meeting delegates the powers and functions of the committee in this behalf. The Chairman or Vice-Chairman is one of the members of the committee and other members are appointed from among the members by the Board at a meeting. However, no member takes part in hearing or determining an application from the ward in which he resides or the ward he represents. An application cannot be heard or determined by the committee unless at least three members including the Chairman or the Vice-Chairman are present. The committee records in brief the reasons for its actions. The decision of the committee or of a majority of the members; or of the officer of Government, is final. An application received after the expiration of one month from the date of publication of the notice relating to the list or after the expiry of fifteen days from the date of service of first notice of demand for payment, is not entertained.

Recovery of Taxes

If any tax payable by owner remains unpaid after the notice has been duly served, and owner is not a resident within the municipality or his place of abode is not known, the amount is recovered from the occupier. Within three months after a tax is due, a notice of demand duly signed by the Chairman, Vice-Chairman or an officer duly authorised, is served upon the concerned person. If any person fails within fifteen days of the notice, either to pay the tax or give sufficient reasons for not paying the amount, the arrear with costs is collected by attachment or sale of any movable property of the defaulter within six months. A penalty at the Rate of $3\frac{1}{8}$ per cent is charged on the arrears with effect from the sixteenth day following the date of service of notice.

Powers and Functions

The Board has mandatory as well as discretionary functions to perform.

Mandatory Functions

The Board is obliged

(1) to establish, maintain and manage cattle pounds;
(2) to regulate line of buildings on public roads and drains;
(3) to prohibit erection or alteration of building without sanction;
(4) to permit construction of latrines and urinals which are to be properly enclosed;
(5) to provide for the removal of sewage, rubbish and offensive matters;
(6) to cause its local area to be inspected frequently to ascertain what nuisances exist calling for abatement and to serve notice to remove the same;
(7) to regulate the establishment of factories, workshops, offensive trades, etc.;
(8) to permit cinemas, dramatic performances, circuses, etc.;
(9) to prohibit private kilns;
(10) to undertake public health works and to formulate and execute schemes to eradicate mosquitoes and to prevent their breeding;
(11) to provide for the registration of births and deaths;
(12) to provide or arrange for the provision of a sufficient supply of drinking water for inhabitants and for other domestic or non-domestic purposes;
(13) to provide and maintain a sufficient and satisfactory system of public drains.

Discretionary Functions and Powers

The Board may

(1) close a public road for repairs;
(2) prohibit use of public road by class of animals or vehicles;
(3) require repair of roads and drains and to declare such roads and drains public;
(4) remove obstructions or encroachments in or on public roads;
(5) require cleansing or lime washing of buildings;
(6) require fencing of building in dangerous state;
(7) require owners to pull down ruins;
(8) provide for drinking water, bathing places, etc.;
(9) require owners to improve bad drainage;
(10) require owners to clear noxious vegetation;
(11) require unwholesome tanks or private premises to be cleansed or drained;
(12) prohibit excavations;
(13) provide and maintain in sufficient number and in proper situation public latrines and urinals;
(14) inspect latrines, privies, cesspools, urinals;
(15) require owner or occupier to repair latrine;
(16) alter any latrine made contrary to orders;
(17) prohibit use of unlicensed markets;
(18) order the use of slaughter houses and the carrying on of dangerous and offensive trades to be discontinued;
(19) establish and maintain fire brigades;
(20) provide places to be used as burial or burning grounds;
(21) grant licenses for the sale at burning grounds of fuel and other articles used for cremation of dead bodies;
(22) prohibit the keeping of the brothels and the residence of a public prostitute;
(23) establish, maintain and manage of any school other than basic schools;
(24) establish and maintain dispensaries, hospitals, chest clinics, asylums and places for the reception of sick or destitutes or contribute towards the cost of the establishment and maintenance of such institutions;
(25) establish and maintain Maternity Homes and child welfare centres.

Control in Respect of Public Health

The Director of Health Services recommends for adoption by the Municipal Boards, such measures as are necessary for improving the public health administration or for safeguarding the public health. The District or the Sub-Divisional Medical Officer of Health regularly but not less than twice a year inspects the different areas and sends reports to the Municipal Boards and to the Director of Health Services.

The Board considers the notes at its meeting and submits a report of the action taken or proposed to be taken to the State Government through the Director of Health Services. The Assistant Director of Public Health also makes inspections and submits reports.

Rules and Bye-Laws

The State Government may make rules for the purposes of carrying out the provisions of the Act. All rules are subject to the condition of previous publication.

The Board at a meeting specially convened for the purpose may frame bye-laws. The Commissioners of a municipality wholly or in part situated in a hilly tract may at meeting make additional bye-laws for regulating or prohibiting the cutting or destroying of trees or shrub, or the making of excavations or removal of oil or quarrying. The power of framing bye-laws by the Board is subject to the previous publication. No such bye-law come into force until it has been confirmed by the State Government and published thereafter. The State Government may cancel their confirmation and thereupon the bye-laws cease to have effect.

The Board, at a special meeting convened for the purpose, may make subsidiary rules as to business and affairs. These subsidiary rules are subject to the sanction of the State Government and thereafter its publication brings them in force.

Delegation of Powers

The powers and functions of the State Government may be delegated to the Commissioner of the Division. Such a delegation has to be notified.

Appeals

Any person aggrieved by the refusal of the Board to sanction the erection of any building or by a notice from the Board requiring a road to be drained, levelled, paved, flagged, metalled or provided with proper lighting or requiring the alteration or demolition of a building or by any orders made by the Board may appeal within thirty days from the date of refusal, notice or order to the Board. Every such appeal can be heard and determined by not less than three members of the Board. These members are appointed by the Board at a meeting. No such refusal, notice or order is liable to be called in question otherwise than by such an appeal. The appellate authority may for sufficient cause extend the period of thirty days. The order of the appellate authority is final.

A person aggrieved by an order refusing a licence or permission may within thirty days appeal to the State Government or an officer authorised by the State Government in that behalf, whose decision is final and cannot be questioned in any court.

Control

The Commissioner of the Division, the Deputy Commissioner, the Director of Municipal Administration, the Sub-Divisional Officer or any other officer specially appointed by the State Government, by general or special order, may at all times, enter into and inspect, or cause any other person to enter into and inspect any municipal office and affairs of or any immovable property in the occupation of or any work in progress under or any institution under the control and administration of the Board, and call for and inspect any book or document which may be in possession or under the control of the Board.

Any Commissioner, with the previous sanction of the Chairman, may inspect any work or institution, constructed or maintained in whole or in part at the expense of the Board and any register, books, accounts or other documents belonging to or in the possession of the Board.

The State Government may appoint an officer of the Government to be Inspector of Municipal Works for one or more municipalities. He performs such duties and exercises such powers as may be assigned to him by rule. He may at all times enter upon or into and inspect any immovable property in the occupation, or any work in progress, under the orders of the Board of any municipality and the Board has to furnish such statements, estimates and reports as he may require. A report of every inspection is prepared and a copy thereof is forwarded by him to the Board. The Board in all matters of professional details is guided by his report.

The State Government, the Commissioner of Division, the Deputy Commissioner, the Director of Municipal Administration, the Additional Deputy Commissioner or the Sub-Divisional Officer may, by order in writing, suspend the execution of any resolution or order of the Board, or prohibit the doing of any act, if in its or his opinion, the resolution, order or act militates against the fundamental rights conferred under the Constitution and the State Policy on the Directive Principles, or is in excess of the powers conferred by law or the execution of the resolution or order, or the doing of the act is likely to lead to a serious breach of peace, or to cause serious injury or annoyance to the public or to any class or body of persons. When the Commissioner of Division or the Deputy Commissioner or the Director of Municipal Administration or the Additional Deputy Commissioner or the Sub-Divisional Officer, makes any order, he forthwith forwards a copy thereof with a statement of his reasons for making it, to the State Government. The State Government may thereupon rescind the order or direct that it continues in force with or without modification, permanently or for such period as it thinks fit.

The State Government may by order in writing, annul any proceedings which it considers not to be in conformity with the law and may do all things necessary to secure such conformity. Such an order is not made without giving the Board an opportunity of expressing its views on the matter.

On receipt of a complaint or information, if it appears to the State Government that the Board has made default in performing any duty imposed on them, the State Government may, by an order in writing, call upon the Board to perform the duty within stipulated period of time. If such duty is not performed, the State Government may, after considering any representation of the Board, either revoke or modify the order or appoint some fit and proper person to perform the duty.

In case of any emergency if the Deputy Commissioner upon the recommendation of the technical adviser is of the opinion that the immediate execution of any work or immediate doing of any act is necessary for the health or safety of the public, he may call upon the Board to execute the work. If such work is not executed within the stipulated period, he may appoint some fit and proper person to execute the work or do the act immediately. The Deputy Commissioner forthwith reports to the Commissioner of the Division who may pass such orders as he thinks fit. The expenses incurred on performing such duty or executing the work or doing the act are paid out of the municipal fund. The Board may prefer an appeal to the State Government against the decision of the Commissioner of the Division as regards assessment of expenses and remuneration.

Dissolution

If, in the opinion of the State Government, a Board is not competent to perform, or persistently makes default in the performance of the duties imposed on the Board, or exceeds or abuses its power, or in the event of failure on the part of the Board to provide such services declared by the State Government in the Official Gazette as the essential services, the State Government may by notification stating the reasons for doing, declare the Board to be incompetent or in default or to have exceeded or abused its powers, and dissolve the Board. The Board is however given a reasonable opportunity of being heard before dissolution.

After dissolution, the State Government appoints an officer to perform all duties and exercise all powers of the Board. Such an officer obtains prior approval of the Director of Municipal Administration in the matter on which the decision of the Board is necessary.

MUNICIPAL CORPORATION

There is a Corporation charged with the Municipal Administration of the city of Guwahati. It is a body corporate and has perpetual succession and a common seal and may sue and be sued.

Constitution

The Corporation consists of

(i) *Elected Councillors*
One councillor for every population of 15,000 subject to a maximum of 60;

(ii) *Appointed Members*
The State Government may nominate persons having special knowledge or experience in Municipal Administration;

(iii) *Ex-officio Members*
(a) MPs and MLAs representing the constituencies which comprise fully or partly the Corporation; and
(b) The members of the Council of States registered as electors within the Corporation area.

The nominated members have the right to attend the meetings but cannot vote.

Reservation

The seats in the Corporation are reserved as under:

(i) For the Scheduled Castes and the Scheduled Tribes in proportion of their population in the total population;

(ii) For the women belonging to the Scheduled Castes and Scheduled Tribes, to the extent of one-third of the seats reserved for those classes;

(iii) For the women to the extent of one-third.

Disqualifications for Councillorship

A person is disqualified for being chosen as, and for being, a councillor on the following grounds :

(i) if he is of unsound mind and stands so declared by a competent court;

(ii) if he is an undischarged insolvent;

(iii) if he is not a citizen of India, or has voluntarily acquired the citizenship of a foreign state or is under any acknowledgement of allegiance or adherence to a foreign state;

(iv) if he has been found to be guilty of any corrupt practice or any offence punishable under the Indian Penal Code;

(v) if he holds any office of profit under the Government or under the Corporation or under any other local authority;

(vi) if he has been sentenced on conviction by a criminal court to imprisonment;

(vii) if he is directly interested in any subsisting contract made with or any work being done for the Corporation except as a shareholder in an incorporated company or as a member of a cooperative society;

(viii) if he is retained or employed in any professional capacity either personally or in the name of a firm of which he is a partner or with which he is engaged in a professional capacity in connection with any cause or proceedings in which the Corporation or any of the municipal authorities is interested or concerned;

(ix) if he fails to pay any arrears due from him to the Corporation within three months after a notice in this behalf has been served upon him;

(x) if he absents himself during three successive months from the meetings of the Corporation except from temporary illness or other cause to be approved by the Corporation;

(xi) if he absents himself from or is unable to attend, the meetings of the Corporation during the successive meetings for any cause whether approved by the Corporation or not.

Resignation by Councillors

A Councillor may by writing under his hand addressed to the Mayor resign his office. Such a resignation takes effect from the date on which it is accepted by the Mayor.

Powers of Councillors

Any Councillor may call the attention of the proper Municipal Authority to any neglect in the execution of the municipal works, to any waste of municipal property or to the wants of any locality and may suggest any improvements. Every Councillor has the right to interpellate the Mayor on matters connected with the Municipal Administration.

Mayor and Deputy Mayor

The Corporation has to elect at its first meeting after the first day of January every year one of its members to be the Mayor and one of the members as Deputy Mayor from amongst its members. The Mayor or the Deputy Mayor is entitled to hold office from the time of his election and until the election of his successor. On the occurrence of any vacancy, the Corporation at its next meeting elects a successor who is entitled to hold office during the remainder of the term.

The Mayor is the head of the Corporation and is responsible to the Corporation. He has full access to all the records of the Corporation and can obtain reports from the Commissioner on any matter. Every correspondence by the Commissioner to the Government or other authority is sent under intimation to the Mayor and on such intimation the Mayor may furnish his views to the Government.

The Mayor presides over all the meetings of the Corporation. His decision and rulings in conducting the proceedings of the meetings are final. He is solely responsible for maintenance of discipline in the meetings of the Corporation.

When the office of the Mayor is vacant, his functions devolve upon the Deputy Mayor until a new Mayor is elected. When the Mayor is absent from his duty on account of illness or any other cause, the powers, duties and functions of the Mayor are exercised and performed by the Deputy Mayor. The Mayor may delegate any of his functions to the Deputy Mayor.

The Mayor may resign his office by giving notice in writing to the Corporation and his resignation takes effect from the date on which it is placed before the Corporation. The Deputy Mayor may resign his office by giving notice in writing to the Mayor and his resignation takes effect from the date on which it is received by the Mayor.

Election Petition

An election can be questioned only by presenting a petition to the prescribed authority within forty-five days from the date on which the result of the election is notified. The petition should contain concise statement of the internal facts and sufficient particulars set forth the grounds on which the election is questioned. It is accompanied by a sum of Rs. 250 as security. The petition is tried and disposed of by the District Judge. The District Judge after announcing orders sends a copy thereof to the Corporation and the Government.

An appeal can lie from every order passed by the District Judge. Such an appeal can be preferred within a period of forty-five days from the date of the order of the District Judge. The decision of the High Court on an appeal is final and conclusive.

Standing Committee

There are Standing Committees dealing with

(i) Taxation and Finance, and Planning and Development (or Standing Finance Committee).
(ii) Public Works,
(iii) Public Health, Conservancy and Water Supply,
(iv) Assessment, Markets and Trades,
(v) Appeals.

Each Standing Committee consists of five members elected by the Corporation at its first meeting after the first day of January every year, from its own members other than the Mayor. No Councillor can be a member of more than one Committee at the same time. Where a vacancy occurs in Standing Committee, the Corporation has to fill up the vacancy as soon as may be, by the election of another Councillor.

Every Standing Committee at its first meeting elects one of its members to be the Chairman and another as its Deputy Chairman. The Chairman and Deputy Chairman holds office from the time of his election until the election of his successor. The outgoing Chairman or Deputy Chairman is eligible for re-election. The Chairman or the Deputy Chairman or any other member of the Standing Committee may resign by writing under his hand addressed to the Mayor.

The Corporation can by regulations determine the powers and duties of each Standing Committee. It may provide for a conference of the two or more Standing Committees or a Joint Committee for any purpose of joint interest. The Standing Committee dealing with finance and taxation, in addition to the powers, duties and functions determined under regulations, can supervise the utilisation of the budget grant, and has access to the accounts of the Corporation and may require the Commissioner to furnish any explanation. It may conduct a monthly audit of the municipal accounts and is bound to check the monthly abstract of receipts and disbursements for the preceding months as furnished by the Commissioner. It may also recommend to the Corporation the writing off of the amount of any loss of, or of any depreciation caused to municipal property which appears to the Committee to be irrecoverable.

The Committee may by resolution in writing, authorise the Commissioner to take action in anticipation of its approval, sanction, consent or concurrence.

The Standing Committees gives effect to every resolution of the Corporation.

Joint Committee

The Corporation may, and if so required by the Government, join with a local authority or authorities in appointing a Joint Committee for any purpose of joint interest and responsibility. Such a committee may include persons who are not members of the local authorities concerned but who may possess special qualifications for serving on such committee. However, the number of such persons cannot exceed one-third of the total number of members of the committee.

Special Committee

The Corporation may by specific resolution, constitute a Special Committee to enquire into and report upon any matter to be specified in resolution, which may arise in connection with any of the powers, duties and functions of the Corporation and which is not at the time under consideration by Standing Committee.

Every Special Committee has to conform to any instructions given to it by the Corporation. The Corporation may dissolve or alter the constitution of any Special Committee, and may withdraw from any Special Committee any of the powers, duties and functions delegated to it. In the absence of the Chairman, the members choose one of themselves to preside over the meeting, the report of every Special Committee is laid before the Corporation which may take action or may refer back the matter to the Special Committee for further investigation and report.

Transaction of Business

The Corporation has to meet atleast once a month for the transaction of business. The Mayor or, in his absence the Deputy Mayor may and has to, upon a requisition made in writing by any 15 Councillors, call a meeting of the Corporation. The first meeting of the Corporation after the general election is held as early as possible, but not later than six weeks from the date of announcement of the results of the election. The first meeting is convened by the District Magistrate (Executive).

A notice of meeting alongwith a list of business to be transacted has to be delivered at registered address of each Councillor at least five days before the time fixed for such meeting. No other business can be transacted at the meeting. However, any Councillor may send or deliver to the Municipal Secretary notice of any other resolution so as to reach him atleast three days before the date fixed for the meeting. The Municipal Secretary has to take steps to circulate such resolution to every Councillor.

The Mayor or in his absence, the Deputy Mayor presides at every meeting of the Corporation. He has a second vote in all cases of equality of votes. His ruling in conducting the proceeding of the meeting is final. In absence of both, the Councillors present at the meeting choose one of themselves to preside. A meeting for election of the Mayor and the Deputy Mayor is presided over by the Commissioner of the Plains Division, but he has no vote. In case of equality of votes, the determination is made by lot, to be drawn in the meeting. The presiding officer reports to the State Government the name of the person elected as Mayor or Deputy Mayor and the State Government publishes it in the official gazette.

A business cannot be transacted at any meeting unless such meeting has been called by the Mayor or Deputy Mayor or by a person authorised to sign a requisition or when a quorum is not present. The quorum at a meeting is one-half of the total number of Councillors of the Corporation when any of the following business is to be disposed of:

(i) Scale of establishment and salaries,
(ii) The framing of regulations and bye-laws,
(iii) The annual budget estimate,
(iv) The appointment or the fixing of the pay or allowances of a paid Secretary, Engineer, Water Works Superintendent, Health Officer, Assessor or other officers,
(v) Imposition of taxes, fees and tolls,
(vi) The election of Mayor or Deputy Mayor or members of the Standing Committees.
(vii) Raising of a loan,
(viii) The subject of a meeting specially convened for the purpose,
(ix) Any other subject prescribed by regulations and bye-laws framed in this behalf.

For all other business, the quorum is one-third of the total number of Councillors. If at any meeting the prescribed quorum is not present, the meeting stands adjourned to a future day to be appointed by the Mayor and three days' notice of an adjourned meeting is given. At such adjourned meeting the Councillors present form a quorum.

All matters are determined by a majority of the Councillors voting at the meeting. The voting is done by show of hands provided the Corporation resolves that any question should be decided by ballot. At any meeting, unless a poll is demanded by at least five members, a declaration by the presiding officer that a resolution has been carried or lost and an entry to that effect in the minutes, is conclusive evidence. If a poll is demanded, the polls of all the members present who desire to vote are taken under the direction of the Presiding Officer. The result of such poll is deemed to be the decision of the Corporation at such meeting.

If a Councillor has any pecuniary interest, direct or indirect, in any contract or employment or other matter and is present in a meeting at which the matter is the subject of consideration, he discloses the fact at the commencement of the meeting and cannot take part in the consideration or vote on any question with respect to the matter. The Municipal Secretary records in a book to be kept for the purpose, particulars of any disclosure and of any notice.

The book remains open at all reasonable hours for the inspection of any Councillor.

Every meeting is open to public, unless a majority of the Councillors present at the meeting decide by resolution that any enquiry or deliberation pending before the Corporation is held in private. The Corporation may make rules for regulating the admission of the members of the public to its meetings and for the removal by force of any member of the public admitted to a meeting for interrupting or disturbing the proceedings of the meeting.

The Chairman or, in his absence, the Deputy Chairman presides every meeting of a Standing Committee, in the absence of the Chairman and the Deputy Chairman, the members choose one of themselves to preside over the meeting. The Corporation makes rules for regulating the conduct of business at meetings of Standing Committee and Special Committees as also Sub-Committees and Joint Committees.

Any Standing Committee, Special Committee or Joint Committee may appoint one or more Sub-Committees for any purpose with which it is entitled to deal and which can be more usefully carried out by a Sub-Committee. All proceedings of any Sub-Committee are subject to confirmation by the committee appointing it.

Minutes of each meeting are drawn up and entered in a book kept for that purpose duly signed by the presiding officer and are laid before the next meeting of the Corporation or of such Committees for confirmation. Copies of the proceedings of each meeting are circulated amongst the members well ahead of the next meeting. The Commissioner forwards to the State Government a copy of the minutes of the proceedings of each meeting of the Corporation, within ten days from the date on which the minutes of the proceedings were signed.

Commissioner

The Commissioner may, in case of emergency, direct the execution of any work or doing of any act which ordinarily requires the approval, sanction, concurrence or consent of the Corporation or the Mayor and the immediate execution or doing of which is necessary for service or safety of the public or for the prevention of extensive damage to any property of the Corporation, and, may direct that expenses incurred are paid from the Municipal Fund. The Commissioner has to report forthwith to the Mayor, the action taken and the reasons thereof.

The Commissioner is responsible for the custody of all records of the Corporation including all papers and documents connected with the proceedings of the Corporation, the Standing Committees and other Committees.

The Commissioner may delegate to the holder of any municipal office any of his ordinary powers, duties or functions. Such delegation is reported to the Mayor. Whenever the Commissioner takes any action in anticipation of the approval, sanction, consent or concurrence of the Corporation, he has to inform the Mayor forthwith. The Commissioner may, on his own responsibility and by an order in writing, authorise the Health Officer, the Engineer, the Revenue Officer, or any other officer who is the head of a department working under the Commissioner, or any person in temporary charge of the duties of any of the officers, exercise the emergency powers conferred upon him.

The Commissioner cannot grant leave of absence for any period exceeding one month to any municipal officer or staff not appointed by him without obtaining the sanction of the Standing Finance Committee.

Municipal Officers

The Corporation may appoint proper persons including officers on deputation from State Government to be the Chief Engineer, the Collector, the Chief Accounts and Audit Officer, the Chief Health Officer, the Municipal Secretary and on other posts. The qualifications, salary, allowances, the period of probation, the period of service, the age of superannuation and all other conditions of service of officers are prescribed by rules made by the Corporation. The appointment of every such officer is subject to the approval of the State Government. If the State Government does not communicate its approval to the appointment of any officer within 45 days from the date of receipt of the communications from the Corporation, the appointment is deemed to have been approved. If the State Government refuses to approve the appointment, the Corporation can make a fresh appointment to the post within forty five days from the date of receipt of the communication refusing such approval. In the event of the failure of the Corporation to make a fresh appointment within the stipulated period of time, the State Government may appoint a person to the post.

Municipal Secretary

The Municipal Secretary is the Secretary of the Corporation and also of the Standing Committee. He can perform such duties as he is directed to perform and is required by the Corporation and the Standing Committee.

He has the custody of all papers and documents connected with the proceedings of the Corporation and any Committee or Standing Committee. He can prescribe the duties of the officers and employees immediately subordinate to him, and subject to the orders of the Standing Committee, can exercise supervision and control on the acts and proceedings of the officers and employees and dispose of all questions relating to service remuneration and privileges of the officers and employees.

Corporation Establishment

The Commissioner can prepare and lay before the Standing Finance Committee a schedule setting forth the designation and grades of other officers and servants, who should constitute Corporation establishment indicating the salaries, fees and allowances payable to them. The Standing Finance Committee may either approve or amend such schedule and lay it before the Corporation for its consideration and approval. The Corporation may sanction the schedule with or without modifications and may from time to time amend it either on its own motion or after ascertaining the opinion on the Standing Finance Committee.

Appointment to the Corporation establishment can be made by the Corporation if the maximum salary of the officer is not below Rs. 250 per month and by the Commissioner in all other cases with the approval of the Corporation. Appointment to the above mentioned offices and to posts carrying a maximum salary not below Rs. 1000 per month is made on the recommendation of the Assam Public Service Commission. Appointments to posts carrying maximum salary not below Rs. 250 but below Rs. 1000 per month are made on the recommendation of the Municipal Service Commission. The Municipal Service Commission holds examinations periodically for recommending candidates for appointment to such posts. If the appointing authority proposes that any particular vacancy on such posts should be filled up by the promotion from subordinate ranks, then the Municipal Service Commission decides whether the vacancy should bc filled up by promotion or by direct recruitment and in the latter case invites applications and takes appropriate steps for appointment to the vacancy.

Every Municipal officer and staff may be fined, demoted, suspended or dismissed for any breach of departmental rules or discipline or for carelessness, negligence of duties or other misconduct by the appointing authority. In the case of a Municipal officer or staff drawing a salary not exceeding Rs. 1000 per month and appointed by the Commissioner or by any authority to whom the power of appointment was delegated by the Commissioner, an appeal can lie to the Standing Finance Committee. In the case of a Municipal officer or staff appointed by the Corporation on the recommendation of the Municipal Service Commission or the Assam Public Service Commission, an appeal can lie to the State Government.

However, it is not necessary to consult the Public Service Commission and the Municipal Service Commission, where a vacancy is not likely to exceed three months or if the post is created for temporary period not likely to exceed six months.

Municipal Service Commission

The Corporation has to constitute a Municipal Service Commission consisting of a Chairman, who should be member of the State Public Service Commission deputed from time to time, the Secretary to the State Government in the Department of Municipal Administration or his nominee and two Councillors selected by the Corporation.

The Corporation has to provide for the manner in which the

Commission should perform the duties and the number of members of the staff and their conditions of service.

Powers of the Corporation

It is incumbent on the Corporation to make adequate provision for each of the following matters:

(i) the construction, maintenance and cleaning of drains and drainage works and public latrines, urinals and similar conveniences,

(ii) the construction and maintenance of works and means for providing a supply of water for public and private purposes.

(iii) the scavenging, removal and disposal of filth, rubbish and other obnoxious or polluted matters,

(iv) the reclamation of unhealthy localities, the removal of noxious vegetation and generally the abatement of all nuisances,

(v) the regulation of places for the disposal of the dead and the provision and maintenance of places for the purpose,

(vi) the registration of births and deaths,

(vii) public vaccination and inoculation,

(viii) measures for preventing and checking the spread of dangerous and contagious diseases,

(ix) the establishment and maintenance of hospitals, dispensaries and maternity and child welfare centres and the carrying out of other measures necessary for public medical relief.

(x) the construction and maintenance of municipal markets and slaughter houses and the regulation of all markets and slaughter houses,

(xi) the regulation and abatement of offensive or dangerous trades or practices,

(xii) maintenance of fire brigade and the protection of life and property in case of fire,

(xiii) the securing or removal of dangerous buildings and places,

(xiv) the construction, maintenance, alteration and improvement of public roads, streets, bridges, culverts, causeways and the like,

(xv) the removal of obstructions and projections and unauthorised occupation in or upon streets, bridges and other public places,

(xvi) the naming and numbering of streets and premises, erecting and installing of statues of important personalities,

(xvii) the maintenance of a Municipal Corporation office and all public monuments and open spaces and other property vesting in the Corporation,

(xviii) the establishment and maintenance of cattle pounds,

(xix) the construction and maintenance of residential quarters for the Corporation staff including conservancy staff,

(xx) the maintenance of ambulance service;

(xxi) the provision of public parks, gardens, playgrounds and recreation grounds,

(xxii) the lighting, watering and cleansing of public streets and other public places,

(xxiii) provisions of relief to destitute persons in the city in times of famine and scarcity and the establishment and maintenance of relief works in such time,

(xxiv) taking the measures against food adulteration including milk, ghee, mustard oil, rice, atta and other foodstuff, and

(xxv) the fulfilmert of any other obligation imposed upon the Corporation.

Discretionary Functions

The Corporation may provide solely or partly for all or any of the following matters:

(i) the establishment, aiding or maintenance of educational institutions, libraries, museums, art galleries, botanical or zoological collections,

(ii) the establishment and maintenance of, and aid to stadium, gymnasia and places for sports and games,

(iii) the planting and care of trees on roadsides and elsewhere,

(iv) the survey of buildings and lands,

(v) the registration of marriages,

(vi) the taking of a census of population,

(vii) the civic receptions to persons of distinction,

(viii) the providing of music or other entertainments in public places or places of public resort,

(ix) the holding of fairs and exhibitions,

(x) the organization, maintenance or management of institutions for the care of persons who are destitute, infirm, sick or incurable, or for the care and training of blind, deaf, mute or otherwise disabled persons or of handicapped and uncared for children,

(xi) the organization, maintenance or management of maternity and infant welfare homes or centres,

(xii) the purchase and maintenance of dwelling houses for Corporation employees.

(xiii) any measures for the welfare of the Corporation employees,

(xiv) the organization or management of chemical or bacteriological laboratories for the examination or analysis of water, food adulteration, and drugs for the detection of adulteration or of causes of diseases or for research connected with the public health and medical relief,

(xv) the establishment and maintenance of veterinary hospitals,

(xvi) the organization, construction, maintenance and management of swimming pools, public houses, bathing places and other institutions designed for the improvement of public health,

(xvii) dairying of farms for the supply, distribution and processing of milk products for the benefit of the residents,

(xviii) the provision of milk to expectant or nursing mothers or infants or school children.,

(xix) the construction and maintenance in public street or places, drinking fountains for human and water troughs for animals,

(xx) the regulation of lodging houses, camping grounds and rest houses,

(xxi) the construction, establishment and maintenance of theatres, cinemas, petrol pumps and other public buildings,

(xxii) the organization and maintenance of shops or stalls for meeting the daily necessities of life in times of scarcity,

(xxiii) the prevention of cruelty to animals,

(xxiv) contributions towards public funds raised for the relief of human sufferings or for the public welfare,

(xxv) the acquisition and maintenance of grazing grounds and the establishment and maintenance of breeding stud,

(xxvi) establishing and maintaining a farm or factory for the disposal of sewage,

(xxvii) the constructions and maintenance of warehouses and gardens,

(xxviii) the construction and maintenance of regulation of garages, sheds and stands for vehicles and cattle buyers,

(xxix) the organization and management of cottage industries, handicraft centres and sales emporia,

(xxx) establishing labour welfare centres for its employees and subsidizing the activities of any association, union or club or creche, of such employees, by grant of loans for its general advancement,

(xxxi) the maintenance of a band, orchestra,

(xxxii) establishing or assisting in the establishment of information centres, wherefrom the public may readily obtain information concerning services available within the city,

(xxxiii) arranging for the publication of information or questions relating to Municipal Administration,

(xxxiv) preparing or joining in the preparation or contributions to the cost of preparation of pictures, films, models or exhibitions to be displayed or held,

(xxxv) arranging for the delivery of lectures and addresses and the holding of discussions and arranging for display of books, cinematography, films or models or the holding of exhibitions,

(xxxvi) with the consent of the Government, contributing

towards the expenses of any activities for the purpose of promoting the development of trade, industry or commerce,

(xxxvii) the acquisition of immovable or movable property,

(xxxviii) any measure to promote public safety, health, convenience or general welfare,

(xxxix) the regulation of the trade and commerce,

(xl) the regulation of the distribution of electric power,

(xli) the regulation of streams, *nallas* and pipes carrying water, rubbish and effluents through the city,

(xlii) the doing of anything the expenditure whereof is declared by the Corporation to be an appropriate charge on the Corporation Fund,

(xliii) urban planning including town planning,

(xliv) regulation of land use and construction of buildings,

xlv) planning for economic and social development,

xlvi) slum improvement and upgradation,

xlvii) urban poverty alleviation.

Contracts

Every contract entered into by the Commissioner on behalf of the Corporation is made in the prescribed manner. The common seal of the Corporation is affixed to every contract and every contract is made in writing. The Common seal remains in the custody of the Commissioner.

The Commissioner may sanction any estimate for a particular work not exceeding Rs. 5000. If the amount of estimate exceeds Rs 5000 but does not exceed Rs. 50,000, the Commissioner may sanction the estimate with the approval of the Standing Finance Committee. Where the estimate exceeds Rs. 50,000, the Commissioner causes a detailed report to be prepared and forwards the same to the Standing Committee, which submits the same before the Corporation with its suggestions. The Corporation may reject the project or may approve it either in its entirety or with modifications. Where the Corporation approves the projects, and entire estimated cost exceeds five lakh of rupees, the report is submitted to the State Government. The State Government may approve it or reject it. The work cannot be commenced before the project is sanctioned by the State Government. No material change in the project sanctioned can be carried into effect without the sanction of the State Government.

A contract involving an expenditure exceeding Rs. 10,000 cannot be made by the Commissioner unless it has been sanctioned by the Standing Finance Committee. No contract involving an expenditure exceeding Rs 50,000 can be made by the Commissioner unless it has been sanctioned by the Corporation.

At least seven days before the execution of any work or the supply of any materials or goods which involve an expenditure exceeding Rs. 50,000, the Commissioner gives notice by an advertisement, inviting tenders subject to the approval of the Standing Committee concerned. The Commissioner ordinarily takes sufficient security for due performance of every contract.

Municipal Property

The Corporation has power to acquire and hold movable and immovable property or any interest therein. Whenever the Commissioner is made to acquire any immovable property by agreement, the Government may, upon the application of the Commissioner made with the approval of the Standing Committee, order proceedings to be taken for acquiring on behalf of the Corporation. The Commissioner may in the interest of the Corporation dispose of by sale, letting out on hire or otherwise any movable property of the Corporation not exceeding Rs 1,000 in value in each instance or grant a lease of any immovable property for any period not exceeding twelve months at a time. The Commissioner has to bring all such transactions to the notice of the Standing Committee within 15 days of their execution. With the sanction of the Standing Committee the Commissioner may dispose of by sale, letting out on hire or otherwise any movable property of which the value does not exceed Rs. 5000, and may with the sanction grant a lease of any immovable property for any period exceeding one year or sell or grant a lease in perpetuity of any immoveable property the value or premium whereof does not exceed Rs. 3000. With the sanction of the Corporation, the Commissioner may lease, sell, let out on hire or otherwise any movable property.

Where any immovable property or any right in or over it is claimed by or on behalf of the Corporation or by any person against the Corporation, the Collector may after formal enquiry pass an order deciding the claim. The aggrieved by an order of the Collector may within one year from the date on which the notice was given, institute a suit in any competent Civil court to set aside such order and or to grant a relief in lieu thereof.

All public wells, gates, markets, slaughter houses, manure and night soil depots and public buildings of every description which have been constructed or are maintained by the local authorities prior to the establishment of the Corporation; all public streams, springs and works for the supply, storage and distribution of water for public purposes, and all bridges, buildings, engines, materials and things connected therewith or appertaining thereto and also any adjacent land appertaining to any public land or well; all public sewers and drains and all sewers, drains, culverts and water courses in or under any public street, or constructed by or for the Corporation alongside any public street and all works, materials, things appertaining thereto; all dust, dirt, dung, ashes, refuse, animal matter or filth or rubbish of any kind or dead bodies of animals collected by the Corporation from the streets, houses, privies, sewers, cesspools or elsewhere or deposited in places fixed by the Corporation; all public lamps, lamp posts, and apparatus connected therewith or appertaining thereto; all land or other property transferred to the Corporation by the Government or acquired by gift, purchase or otherwise for local public purposes; all public streets and the pavements, stones and other materials thereof and also trees growing on and erections, materials, implements and things provided on such streets vest in the Corporation.

The Corporation has to maintain a register and a map of all immovable property which vest in it or which it holds in trust.

The management, control and administration of every public institution maintained out of the Municipal Fund vest in the Corporation. When any public institution has been placed under the direction, management and control of the Corporation, all property and amounts and funds belonging thereto are held by the Corporation in trust.

Municipal Fund

A Municipal Fund is created to which all moneys realized or realizable and all moneys otherwise received by the Corporation are credited. It is held by the Corporation in trust. All moneys payable to the credit of the Municipal Fund are paid into the State Bank of India to the credit of an account styled as "the account of the Municipal Fund of the Corporation".

The moneys are applied in payment of all sums, charges and costs, necessary for carrying out the municipal administration. A payment out of the Municipal Fund can be made only upon a cheque signed by the Commissioner. Except in the case of salaries up to Rs. 300, which are paid in cash, payment of any sum exceeding one hundred rupees is made by a cheque. No payment of any sum is made by the Commissioner unless the expenditure is covered by a current budget grant and a sufficient balance is available.

All investments and deposits are made by the Commissioner with the sanction of the Standing Committee.

Budget

The commissioner in consultation with the Mayor prepares and submits on or before the 15th day of December every year to the Standing Finance Committee, an estimate of the proposed expenditure, an estimate of all balance which will be available expenditure at the commencement of the year, a statement of the proposals as to taxation which will be necessary or expedient to impose, an estimate of receipt from all sources and an estimate of loans to be raised. The Standing Committee considers the estimates and proposals and frames Budget Estimates of the income and expenditure of the Corporation. The Commissioner causes the Budget Estimates as finally approved by the Standing Finance Committee to be printed and not later than the 15th day of February, forwards a copy to each Councillor. The Budget Estimates are laid before the Corporation on the 15th February or as soon as possible thereafter and the Corporation considers the same. It may refer the estimates back to the Standing Committee for further consideration and re-submission within a specified time and adopts on or before the 22nd day of March.

In the Budget Estimates, the Corporation has among other

things to make adequate and suitable provisions for duties imposed upon it, to provide for the payment of all instalments of the principal and interest as they fall due and to allow for a closing balance not less than one lakh rupees.

The Corporation may, on the recommendation of the Standing Finance Committee during the year, increase the amount of the budget grant under any head; make an additional budget grant to meet any special or unforeseen requirement arising during the year; transfer the amount or portion of the amount of the budget grant under any other head and reduce the amount of the budget grant under any head.

If the whole or any part of any budget grant included in the Budget Estimates for a year remains unexpended at the end of the year, and the amount thereof has not been taken into account in the opening balance entered in the Budget Estimate of any of the next two following years, the Standing Finance Committee may sanction the expenditure of such budget grant or the unexpended portion thereof during the next two following years for the completion of the purpose for which the budget grant was originally made and not for any other purpose.

Borrowing

The Corporation may, in pursuance of any resolution passed by it and with the prior approval of the State Government, borrow by way of debentures or otherwise, sums of money which may be required for acquiring any land, for erecting any building, for the execution of any work, the provision of any plant, or the doing of any other things, to pay off any debt due to the Government, to repay a loan previously raised for any other purpose for which the Corporation is authorised to borrow.

Sinking Fund

The Corporation maintains sinking funds for repayment of money borrowed and has to pay every year into such sinking fund an amount sufficient for the repayment within the period fixed for the loan of all moneys borrowed. All money of the sinking fund is invested by the Commissioner in public securities and every such investment is reported by the Commissioner to the Corporation within fifteen days. All dividends and other sums received in respect of any investment is paid into the sinking fund and invested.

Accounts and Audit

The accounts of receipts and expenditure of the Corporation are kept in the manner prescribed by the Standing Finance Committee. The Corporation as soon as the accounts of the past year have been finally passed by it, transmits to the Government a detailed account. The Commissioner as soon as after the first day of April, causes to be prepared a detailed report of the Municipal administration during the previous year, together with a statement showing the amounts of the receipts and disbursements, respectively credited and debited to the Municipal Fund during the previous year, and the balance of the credit at the close of the year. The Commissioner places the report and statement before the Corporation for consideration and forwards a copy thereof to each Councillor and to the Government. The Councillor has to prepare monthly, an abstract of the receipts and expenditure of the month last preceding and places it before the Standing Finance Committee. The Standing Finance Committee has access to all the Municipal accounts and to all records and correspondence. The Commissioner has to furnish to the Standing Finance Committee any explanation concerning receipts and disbursement which it may call for.

The Municipal accounts are audited by or under the order of the Examiner of local accounts. After the completion of the audit, the Examiner prepares a report on the accounts audited and examined and sends a report to the Corporation and a copy to the Government. The Corporation, the Standing Committee or the Commissioner has to forthwith remedy any defects or irregularities reported by the Examiner and have to report to the Government the action taken by the municipal authority concerned. If there is a difference of opinion between the municipal authority and the Examiner or, if the municipal authority does not remedy any defect or irregularity within a reasonable period, the matter is referred to the Government and the Government is competent to pass orders. The orders of the Government are final and the municipal authority has to take action accordingly. If the appropriate action is not taken by the municipal authority within the stipulated period of time, the Government gets it done and the expenses incurred are drawn on the Municipal Fund.

The Examiner may, after giving suitable opportunity of explaining, fix the responsibility and put a surcharge. The Examiner states in writing the reasons for his decision in respect of every disallowance, surcharge or charge and sends a copy by registered post to the person against whom it is made. If the amount is not paid within fourteen days from the period of appeal, the Collector at the request of the Examiner proceeds to recover the amount and have it credited to the Municipal Fund. Any person aggrieved by a disallowance, charge or surcharge made by the Examiner may appeal to the Commissioner of Plains Division. The appellate authority has the power to confirm, vary or quash the decision of the Examiner.

Taxation

The Corporation has power to impose mandatory as well as optional taxes.

Mandatory Taxes

The Corporation can impose

(i) property taxes,
(ii) a tax on draught animals, vessels and vehicles other than those mechanically propelled,
(iii) a tax on theatres, theatrical performance and other shows for public amusements,
(iv) a tax on advertisement other than advertisements published in the newspapers,
(v) a duty on the transfer of property, and
(vi) a tax on professions, trades and calling.

Optional Taxes

The Corporation may levy any or all of the following taxes:

(i) a betterment tax on properties whose value may have increased as a result of town planning scheme undertaken in the city,
(ii) a tax on dogs kept as pets within the city,

(iii) a toll on vehicles and animals entering the city,
(iv) market dues on persons exposing goods for sale in any market or in any space belonging to or under the control of Government or of the Corporation,
(v) a drainage tax where a system of drainage has been introduced,
(vi) a tax on pilgrims resorting periodically to visit shrines within the limits of the Corporation,
(vii) a tax on passengers and goods carried by road or inland waterways,
(viii) a toll on new bridges constructed by the Corporation,
(ix) octroi, and
(x) any other tax with the prior approval of the State Government.

Imposition of Tax

Before the Corporation passes any resolution imposing a tax or duty or fee for the first time, it directs the Commissioner to publish a notice in the Gazette or in the local newspapers, clearly indicating the nature and amount of the tax or duty or fees and the date from which it is proposed to impose the tax. Any resolution abolishing an existing tax or duty or fees or reducing or increasing the rates cannot be carried into effect without the sanction of the Government.

Property Taxes

The property tax is levied on lands and buildings. It consists of

(i) a water tax,
(ii) a scavenging tax,
(iii) a lighting tax, and
(iv) a general tax of not less than ten and not more than twentyfive per cent of the rateable value of lands and buildings.

The corporation may exempt the buildings and lands vesting in the Central Government without the prior approval of the Central Government; building and lands occupied and used for public worship and for charitable purposes and buildings and lands the rental value of which does not exceed twenty five rupees per month, provided the building is occupied by the owner and the owner does not possess any other building or land, the rent of which exceeds twenty five rupees per month in the aggregate.

Water Tax

The water tax can be levied only in respect of lands and buildings to which water supply is made or which are connected by means of pipe from municipal waterworks or which are situated in any portion of the city in which the Commissioner has given public notice that sufficient water is available from municipal waterworks for a reasonable supply to all the lands and buildings in the said portion.

Scavenging Tax

The scavenging tax can be levied only in respect of lands and buildings in which there is a latrine, urinal, cesspool, bathing place or cooking place connected with a municipal drain or which are situated in any portion of the city in which the Commissioner has given public notice that the collection, removal and disposal of all filth and polluted and obnoxious matter from latrines, urinals and cesspools will be undertaken by municipal agency. The Corporation may allow a rebate upto onethird of the scavenging tax on holdings having sanitary latrines.

Rateable Value

The rateable value of any land or building assessable to property taxes is the annual rent at which such land or building might reasonably be expected to be let from year to year less a sum equal to ten per cent of the annual rent allowable in lieu of all allowances for cost of repairs and insurance and necessary to maintain in a state to command that rent and the water tax or the scavenging tax or both, if the rent is inclusive of either or both of the taxes.

The rateable value of any land which is not built upon, but is capable of being built upon and of any land on which a building is in process of erection can be fixed at five per cent of the estimated capital value of such land.

All plants and machinery contained or situated in or upon any land or building and belonging to any of the classes specified by public notice by the Commissioner are deemed to form part of such land or buildings for the purpose of determining the rateable value.

The annual value in case of owner-occupied building and land is deemed to be 25 per cent less than the annual value otherwise determined.

The property taxes are primarily leviable if the land or building is let, upon the lessor; if the land or building is sublet, upon the superior lessor and if the land or building is unlet, upon the person in whom the right to let the same vests.

If any land has been let for a term exceeding one year to a tenant and such tenant has built upon the land, the property taxes assessed in respect of that land and building erected thereon are primarily leviable upon the said tenant, whether the land and building are in the occupation of such tenant or sub-tenant of such tenant. In case of several ownership, the liability is joint or several. The tax in respect of government buildings is payable by the Government and not by the occupier. Property taxes are a first charge on premises on which they are assessed.

Assessment

The Commissioner with the approval of the Standing Committee causes an assessment list of all lands and buildings in the city prepared. After the list is prepared, the Commissioner gives public notice indicating the place where the list may be inspected. Every person is at liberty to inspect the list and to take extracts therefrom free of charges. The Commissioner simultaneously gives public notice of a date not less than one month thereafter, when he will proceed to consider the rateable value of lands and buildings entered in the assessment list. In all cases of first assessment or the assessment is increased, he also gives written notice to the owner or to any lessee or occupier of the land or building. Any objection to a rateable value or assessment has to be made in writing to the Commissioner before the date fixed in the notice. The objections are recorded in a register. All the objections are inquired into and investigated and the persons making them are allowed an opportunity of being heard by the Commissioner or any other officer authorised in this behalf. When all objections are disposed of and the revision of the rateable value and assessment has been completed, the assessment list is authenticated by the signature of the Commissioner. Such an authenticated list is deposited in the office of the Corporation and is open for inspection free of charge. A public notice to this effect is published. The Commissioner with the approval of the Standing Committee may any time amend the assessment list. Before any amendment, the Commissioner has to give to any person affected, notice of not less than one month that an amendment is proposed and considers the objections made by such person.

It is in the discretion of the Commissioner to prepare for the whole or any part of the city a new assessment list every year or to adopt the rateable value and assessment contained in the list. In case of transfer of title, the person whose title is transferred and the person to whom the same is transferred have to give notice of such transfer to the Commissioner within three months after the execution of the instrument of transfer or after its registration or after the transfer is effected, if no instrument is executed. In the event of death of any person primarily liable, the person on whom the title of the deceased devolves has to give notice of such devolution to the Commissioner within six months from the date of death of the deceased. The Commissioner causes every transfer recorded in his books and in the assessment list. On a written request by the Commissioner, the Registrar or Sub-Registrar furnishes particulars regarding the registration of instruments of transfer of immovable properties in the city.

When a new building is erected or when any building is rebuilt or enlarged or when any building is reoccupied, the person primarily liable for the property taxes has to give notice in writing to the Commissioner within fifteen days. The property taxes are assessable on the building from the said date. When any building or portion which is liable to taxes is demolished or removed otherwise than by the order of the Commissioner, the person primarily liable for the payment of taxes has to give notice thereof in writing to the Commissioner. Until such notice is given, the person continues to be liable for payment of taxes.

For determining the rateable value of any land or building, the Commissioner may require the owner or occupier, to furnish him with information or with a written return signed as to the name and place of residence of the owner or occupier, as to the measurements or dimensions of land or building and the rent obtained and as to the actual cost or other specified details connected with the determination of the value of land or building. Every person on whom such requisition is made, is bound to comply with and to give true information or to make true return to the best of his knowledge. Whoever omits to comply with or fails to give true information or to make a true return in addition to any penalty, is precluded from objecting to any assessment made by the Commissioner.

Valuers

The Corporation may employ one or more persons to assist the Commissioner in connection with the valuation of any land or building. Any person so employed has power to enter on, survey and value any land or building which the Commissioner may direct him to survey and value.

Duty on Transfer of Property

The Corporation can levy a duty on transfer of immovable property in the form of a surcharge on the duty imposed at rate not exceeding five per cent on the amount specified as under:

(i) Sale of immovable property forth in the instrument	the amount or value of the consideration for the sale
(ii) Exchange of immovable property	the value of the property of the greater value
(iii) Gift of immovable property	the value of the property as set forth in the instrument
(iv) Mortgage with possession of immovable property	the amount secured by the mortgage as set forth in the instrument
(v) Lease in perpetuity of immovable property	the amount equal to one-sixth of the whole amount or value of the rent which would be paid or delivered in respect of the first fifty years of the lease as set forth in the instrument.

The proceeds of the following taxes collected in the city reduced by the cost of collection as determined by the State Government are paid to the Corporation for the performance of its functions:

(i) Land Revenue,
(ii) Local Rates,
(iii) Urban Property Tax,
(iv) Taxes on Entertainment and Betting, and
(v) Tax on Motor Vehicles.

Recovery of Taxes

When any tax has become due, the Commissioner causes to be presented to the person liable for the payment, a bill for the amount due. No bill is prepared in case of a tax on vehicles, boats and animals, a theatre tax and a tax on advertisements. If the amount for which a bill has been presented is not paid within fifteen days, or if the tax on vehicles, boats and animals or the theatre tax or the tax on advertisements is not paid after it has become due, the Commissioner may cause to be served upon the person liable for the payment a notice of demand. For every notice of demand, a fee of such amount not exceeding two rupees is payable by the said person and is included in the cost of recovery. If the person does not pay within thirty days of the service of the notice of demand, and if no appeal is preferred against such tax, he is deemed to be in default. In such case, a sum not exceeding twenty per cent of the amount of the tax may be recovered from him by way of penalty, in addition to the amount of tax and the notice fee. Such an amount may be recovered under a warrant, by distress and sale of the movable property or the attachment and sale of the immovable property of the defaulter. Where the property is in the city, the warrant is addressed to an employee of the Corporation and where the property is outside the city, to the Collector of the district, who can proceed to collect it as arrear of Land Revenue. The employee charged with the execution of warrant of distress, if authorised by the warrant to distrain any movable property or attach any immovable property of the person in default. The property distrained should be, as nearly as possible, equal in value to the amount recoverable under the warrant. The employee makes in the presence of two witnesses, at least one of whom should be a rate-payer, an inventory of the movable property which he seizes and simultaneously gives notice to the person that such property will be sold as mentioned therein. On the expiry of the specified time, the seized property may be sold by public auction under the orders of the Commissioner. The sale proceeds are first applied in discharge of sum due to the Government and secondly, in discharge of the sum due to the Corporation and all incidental costs. The surplus is credited to the Municipal Fund and notice is given to the person to claim the surplus by written application to the Commissioner within one year from the date of the notice. Any surplus not claimed becomes the property of the Corporation.

The Commissioner may with the approval of the Standing Finance Committee write off any sum due on account of any tax or the costs of recovering any tax of such sum which, in his opinion, is irrecoverable.

Remission and Refund

If any building is wholly or partly demolished or destroyed or otherwise deprived of value, the Commissioner may, on the application in writing of the owner or the occupier, remit or refund appropriate portion of any tax. If any building remains vacant and unproductive of rent for a period of at least sixty consecutive days, the Commissioner can remit or refund one-half of the property tax proportionately to the period of the vacancy. A remission or refund can be granted only if notice in writing claiming remission of refund is given to the Commissioner within three months of the beginning of the period for which it is claimed. In no case, any remission or refund is permissible unless the total sum demanded has actually been paid.

The Corporation may, at a meeting, reduce the amount payable on account of any taxes or remit the same on ground of excessive hardship to the person liable to pay the same. Such a reduction or remission can not unless renewed by the Corporation at a meeting have effect for more than one financial year.

Appeals

An appeal against the levy or assessment of any tax lies at the jurisdiction of the Standing Appeal Committee and against the order of the Committee to the Court of the District Judge. If, before or on the hearing of an appeal by District Judge, any question of law arises, the court of the District Judge on its own motion, may or on the application of any party to the appeal, draw up a statement of the facts of the case and refer the statement with its opinion on the question for the decision of the High Court.

An appeal can be heard or determined only if the appeal is, in the case of the property tax, brought within thirty days next after the authentication of the assessment list or within thirty days of the date on which an amendment is finally made and, in the case of any other tax, within thirty days next after the date of the receipt of the notice of assessment or of alteration of assessment or, if no notice is given, within thirty days after the date of the presentation of the first bill or the first notice of demand.

The order of the court in respect of any rateable value or assessment or liability to assessment or taxation is final. The court can review any order passed by it, upon application or on its own motion, in appeal within three months from the date of the order.

Rules, Regulations and Bye-Laws

The Government may make rules for carrying out the municipal administration. All rules are subject to previous publication. Every rule is laid before the State Legislature.

Any regulation which may be made by the Corporation may also be made by the State Government within one year. Any regulation may be altered or rescinded by the Corporation. No regulation made by the Corporation can have effect until it has been approved by the State Government and published in the Official Gazette.

The corporation may make bye-laws on various matters. All the bye-laws are made after previous publication. Copies of all bye-laws are kept at the municipal office and are available for inspection and sale to the public.

Control

The Government may at any time require the Corporation to produce any records, correspondence, plan or other documents in its possession or under its control and to furnish any return, plan, estimate, statement, accounts or statistics relating to the proceedings, duties or works of the Corporation of any of the Corporation or any of the municipal authorities and to furnish or obtain and furnish any report. The Government may depute any Government employee to inspect or examine any municipal office, work or thing and report thereon. The Government may after consideration of any representation which may be made by the Corporation, by written order, annul or omit from the records any proceedings of the Corporation which it considers not to be in conformity with the Act or any rules or bye-laws. If the Government is of the opinion that the execution of any resolution or order of the Corporation or any other municipal authority or employee or the doing of any act which is about to be done or is being done by or on behalf of the Corporation is in contravention of or in exercise of the powers conferred by the Act or of any other law or is likely to lead to a breach of peace or to cause injury or annoyance to the public or to any class or body of persons, the Government may, by order, in writing, suspend the execution of such resolution or order, or prohibit the doing of any such act.

WARDS COMMITTEES

In a municipality having a population of three lakhs or more, Ward Committees are constituted. A Ward Committee consists of one or more wards but not more than four wards. The area of Wards Committee is notified by the State Government within three months from the date of receipt of proposals in this regard from the concerned Board/Corporation.

The total number of members of each Wards Committee should not be more than eight, consisting of four Ward Commissioners and four other representing interest groups, leading citizen who may be nominated by the Deputy Commissioner in case of municipalities and by the Government in the Corporation.

The Chairman is elected from amongst the elected members of the Ward Committee.

The Wards Committee mainly looks after the needs of the residents in a more intimate manner making it unnecessary for the residents to go to the Municipality or Corporation. The decision of the Ward Committee with regard to selection of schemes for development in the area is binding on the part of the Municipality in which such schemes are taken up for execution by the Board. The tenure of the Wards Committee is coterminous with the tenure of the Board or Corporation.

State Finance Commission

The Assam Municipal Act, 1956 and the Guwahati Municipal Corporation Act, 1969 make mention of the Finance Commission only in the definition section. Under the provisions of Art. 243I and Art. 243Y of the Constitution of India, the State Government has enacted the Assam Finance Commission (Miscellaneous Provision) Act, 1995 and a four member Commission was set up. The Commission submitted its report in February, 1996.

State Election Commission

The aforementioned Acts include the mention of the Election Commission in their definition sections. They provide for the constitution of the State Election Commission as referred to in the Constitution of India.

LIST OF TOWNS

Name of Town	*Population (1991)*	*Growth Rate (1971-81)*	*1981-91)*
(1)	*(2)*	*(3)*	*(4)*
1. Guwahati	5,77,591	-	188.25
2. Dibrugarh	1,23,885	-	54.19
3. Silchar	1,15,045	-	118.73
4. Jorhat	1,11,584	-	57.89
5. Nagaon	93,324	-	65.07
6. Tinsukia	73,760	-	34.33
7. Dhubri	65,861	-	44.47
8. Tezpur	54,999	-	37.95
9. Bongaigaon	48,907	-	96.02
10. Lumding	46.064	-	57.47
11. Karimganj	43,623	-	37.97

(1)	*(2)*	*(3)*	*(4)*
12. North Lakhimpur	40,044	-	99.28
13. Diphu	39.551	-	287.75
14. Goalpara	39,208	-	134.74
15. Sibsagar	36.651	-	33.64
16. Digboi	35,930	-	10.94
17. Hojai	31,916	-	40.17
18. Barpeta Road	29,831	-	75.50
19. Golaghat	28,722	-	54.50
20. Kokrajhar	28,240	-	65.53
21. Haflong	26.191	-	403.96
22. Haita Kandi	25,475	-	53.06
23. Barpeta	25,345	-	(-)4.20
24. Mankachar	22,739	-	84.14
25. Marghevita	21.692	-	134.51
26. Mariani	20,941	-	39.11
27. Rangia	20,912	-	111.98
28. Mangaldai	20,720	-	70.53
29. Gaunpur	19,945	-	55.21
30. Namrup	19,684	-	146.91
31. Lanka	19,044	-	-
32. Nalbari	18,949	-	51.01
33. Rangapara	18,526	-	54.72
34. Bilasipara	17,994	-	43.34
35. Marigaon	17,246	-	-
36. Duliajan Oil town	16,852	-	46.58
37. Badarpur	16,490	-	(-)16.29
38. Chapar	16,253	-	-
39. Tangla	15,814	-	65.21
40. Dhekiajuli	15,469	-	84.25
41. Kharupatia	15,343	-	46.85
42. Doom Dooma	15,038	-	43.08
43. Naharkatia	15,037	-	39.57
44. Biswanath Chavali	14,586	-	56.82
45. Snalkuchi	14,290	-	3.75
46. Jagirvad	13,582	-	-
47. Niz Hajo	12,781	-	24.46
48. Sapatgram	12,629	-	27.84
49. North Guwahati	12,426	-	59.80

(1)	*(2)*	*(3)*	*(4)*
50. Howli	12,402	-	59.33
51. Sonari	12,263	-	402.99
52. Dergaon	12,200	-	22.34
53. Udalguri	12,077	-	-
54. Makum	11,984	-	100.00
55. Abhayapuri	11,686	-	66.23
56. Dhing	11,469	-	6.41
57. Gassaingaon	11,316	-	-
58. Bijni	11,313	-	41.43
59. Barugaon	11,126	-	-
60. Bokajan	11,008	-	-
61. Lakhipur	8,991	-	68.62
62. Dhemaji	8,826	-	-
63. Lala	8,631	-	55.91
64. Bihpuria	8,506	-	61.83
65. Nazira	8,336	-	54.20
66. Donkamokam	8,147	-	-
67. Sarthebari	7,705	-	19.03
68. Bohari	7,583	-	-
69. Pathsala	7,236	-	44.11
70. Sorbhog	7,176	-	19.86
71. Bokakhat	6,997	-	-
72. Golokganj	6,220	-	-
73. Chabua	6,032	-	55.14
74. Maibong	5,802	-	-
75. Amingaon	5,586	-	26.58
76. Palasbari	4,683	-	12.52
77. Tehu	4,290	-	32.24
78. Dokmoka	4,091	-	-
79. Moranhat	3,978	-	57.61
80. Jagirvad Paper Mill	3,790	-	-
81. Raha	3,777	-	-
82. Hamran	3,771	-	-
83. Lakhipur	3,748	-	27.44
84. Howraghat	3,781	-	-
85. Amguri	3,583	-	43.55
86. Mahur	2,213	-	-
87. Jogighopa	1,927	-	-

THREE

Manipur

In pursuance of the Fifth Schedule of the Constitution, the Indian Parliament enacted the Manipur Municipalities Act, 1994 to provide for constitution and organization of municipalities in the urban areas of the State. The Act extends to the whole of the State excepting the Hill areas to which the Manipur (Hill Areas) District Council Act, 1971 applies.

Constitution of Municipalities

The Governor may declare the constitution of

(a) a Nagar Panchayat for a transitional area,
(b) a Municipal Council for a smaller urban area, and
(c) a Municipal Corporation for a larger urban area.

Before issuing a notification for constituting a municipality, a draft of the notification is published indicating local limits of the area. Any inhabitant of the area may object to the notification in writing to the Deputy Commissioner within 45 days from the date of publication of the notification. The Deputy Commissioner shall within 45 days of the receipt of the objection, forward the same with his comments to the Government for its consideration.

Composition of Municipalities

Every Municipal Council and Nagar Panchayat consists of such number of councillors as is fixed by the State Government. It consists of:

(a) Elected Councillor : All seats are filled by persons chosen by direct election;
(b) Appointed Councillor : The Government may appoint a person

having special knowledge or experience in municipal administration.

The Appointed Councillor does not have right to vote in the meetings.

Reservation

In every municipality, the State Government makes reservation:

(i) to the Scheduled Castes and the Scheduled Tribes in proportion of their population to the total population;
(ii) not less than one-third of the total number of seats reserved for the Scheduled Castes and the Scheduled Tribes for women belonging to such classes;
(iii) not less than one-third of seats to women.

Chairperson and Vice-Chairperson

Every Council or a Nagar Panchayat has a Chairperson and a Vice-Chairperson. The Councillors at the first meeting, to be called at the instance of the Deputy Commissioner, elect one of them to be the Chairperson. Such an election has to be completed within 21 days from the date of notification of the result. In case of any vacancy in the office of the Chairperson, a new Chairperson is elected within 21 days from the date of the occurrence of the vacancy. The State Government appoints a person to preside over such a meeting. The Councillors either at the first or at any subsequent meeting elect one of them to be a Vice-Chairperson.

Resignation

The Chairperson of a Nagar Panchayat may resign his office by writing under his hand addressed to the Executive Officer. The Vice-Chairperson or a councillor may resign his office by writing under his hand addressed to the Chairperson who shall forward it to the Executive Officer. The Executive Officer forthwith intimates the fact of resignation to the Nagar Panchayat and the State Government. On receipt of intimation, the State Government notifies the fact of the resignation and occurrence of casual vacancy. The resignation takes effect from the date on which it is accepted by the State Government.

The Chairperson of Municipal Council may resign his office by writing a resignation letter addressed to the Vice-Chairperson, who delivers the letter to the Executive Officer. The Vice-Chairperson or a Councillor may resign his office by writing a letter of resignation addressed to the Chairperson, who forthwith delivers the letter to the Executive Officer. The Executive Officer intimates the fact of resignation to the Council and the State Government. On receipt of the intimation, the State Government notifies the same in the Official Gazette and the resignation comes into effect.

Removal of Councillors

The State Government may remove any elected Councillor on the ground of his misconduct in the discharge of his duties, if the removal is recommended by a resolution of the municipality passed at a special meeting and supported by a majority of not less than two-thirds of Councillors present and voting in such a meting OR if he ceases to reside within the municipality continuously for a period of twelve months OR if he has been declared by notification to have violated his oath or affirmation of allegiance OR if he has disqualified by or under any law for electing to the State Legislative Assembly, OR if he has knowingly acquired or continued to hold without the permission in writing of the State Government directly or indirectly or as a partner, any share of interest in any contract or employment with, by or on behalf of the municipality, OR if he is in arrears of any dues to the municipality for more than six months after a bill or a notice has been duly served on him.

No-Confidence Motion against Chairperson or Vice-Chairperson

The State Government may remove by a notification in the Official Gazette, from office , the Chairperson or the Vice-Chairperson, in pursuance of a resolution passed by a majority of the total number of the Councillors and supported by not less than two-thirds of the Councillors present and voting at a meeting specially convened for the purpose. Such a meeting can be convened by the Executive Officer on requisition signed by not less than one-fifth of the total number of Councillors constituting the Nagar Panchayat or the Council for the time being. The notice of meeting signifying the time and the place thereof is despatched by the Executive Officer to every Councillor ten days prior the meeting. The Chairperson or the Vice-Chairperson against whom the resolution is to be moved, does not preside over the meeting. A copy of the notice is sent to the State Government. The removal becomes effective from the date of its resolution in this regard.

Removal of Chairperson or Vice-Chairperson

If a Chairperson or a Vice-Chairperson remains absent from office owing to illness or any other cause for a period exceeding three months without the leave of the Nagar Panchayat or the Council, he ceases functioning on the post and his office becomes vacant.

Powers and Functions of the Chairperson

The Chairperson presides over all the meetings of the Nagar Panchayat or the Council and watches over the financial and executive administration of the municipality and exercises supervisory and executive control over acts and duties of all officers and employees of the Nagar Panchayat or the Council, in matters respecting their executive functions and the accounts and records of the Nagar Panchayat or the Council. He also directs, in case of emergency, the execution or stoppage of any work or doing of any act, which requires the sanction of the Nagar Panchayat or the Council and the immediate execution or doing of which is necessary for the service or safety of the public, and expenses incurred are paid from the Municipal Fund. Such an action, however, is reported by him and the reasons therefor to the Nagar Panchayat or the Council at its next meeting.

Functions of Vice-Chairperson

It is the function of the Vice-Chairperson, in the absence of the Chairperson, to preside over the meeting of the Nagar Panchayat or the Council. He exercises the same authority as is vested in the Chairperson. The Vice-Chairperson exercises the powers and performs the duties of the Chairperson, pending the election of the Chairperson.

Powers of Municipality

The State Government may, by notification, entrust the municipalities with the function of the preparation of plans for economic development and social justice, and the performance of functions and the implementation of schemes including those in relation to the matters listed in the Schedule XII of the Constitution.

Functions of the Municipality

The municipalities in the State are entrusted with obligatory as well as discretionary functions delineated as under :

Obligatory Functions

Every municipality is obliged to perform the following functions:

(i) lighting public roads and places,
(ii) watering public roads and places,
(iii) cleaning public roads, places and sewers,
(iv) removing noxious vegetation,
(v) abating all public nuisance,
(vi) extinguishing fires and protecting life and property when fire occurs,
(vii) removing filth, rubbish, nightsoil, bad odour or any other noxious or offensive matters from privies, latrines, urinals, cesspools or other common receptacles for such matter in or pertaining to a building,
(viii) regulating offensive or dangerous trades or practices,
(ix) removing obstructions and projections in public roads or places,
(x) securing or removing dangerous buildings or places,
(xi) reclaiming unhealthy localities,
(xii) acquiring, maintaining, changing and regulating places for the disposal of dead bodies and of the carcasses of dead animals,
(xiii) constructing, altering and maintaining public roads, culverts, municipal boundary marks, markets, slaughter houses, drains, sewers, drainage-works, sewerage-works, baths, washing places, drinking-fountains, tanks, wells, dams and the like,

(xiv) constructing public latrines, privies and urinals,
(xv) obtaining supply of water, proper and sufficient, for preventing danger to the health of inhabitants from the insufficiency or unwholesomeness of the existing supply,
(xvi) naming streets and numbering houses,
(xvii) registering births and deaths,
(xviii) suitable accommodation for any calves, cows or buffaloes required within the municipality for the supply of animal lymph,
(xix) printing annual reports on the administration of the municipality,
(xx) making arrangements for preparation of compost manure from night-soil and rubbish, and
(xxi) establishing and maintaining cattle pounds.

Discretionary Functions

A municipality may at its discretion provide out of the municipal property and fund either wholly or partly, for

(i) laying out new public roads and acquiring land for the purpose,
(ii) constructing, establishing, maintaining or contributing to the maintenance of public parks, gardens, libraries, museums, reading rooms, halls, offices, dharamshalas, rest houses, encamping grounds and other public buildings and places,
(iii) constructing and maintaining suitable sanitary houses for the habitation of the poor and granting loan for the construction of such houses,
(iv) securing or assisting to secure suitable places for the carrying on offensive trades,
(v) providing accommodation for servants employed by the municipality or granting loans to servants for construction of houses,
(vi) planting and maintaining trees on the roadside,
(vii) supplying, construction and maintaining receptacles, fitting pipes and other appliances on or for the use of private premises for receiving and conducting the

sewage into sewers under the control of the municipality,

(viii) the public health and infant welfare,

(ix) contribution towards any public fund raised for the relief of human suffering within and without the municipality,

(x) any public reception, ceremony, entertainment or exhibition within the municipality by a resolution passed at a general meeting and supported by one-half of the total number of Councillors,

(xi) the organization or maintenance of shops or stalls for the sale of necessities of life,

(xii) holding fairs and exhibitions,

(xiii) supply of milk,

(xiv) establishing labour welfare centres for its employees and subsidizing the activity of any association of employees by grant of loan for its advancement,

(xv) maintenance of ambulance service,

(xvi) establishing and maintaining public hospitals and dispensaries and providing public medical service,

(xvii) housing and maintaining destitute, orphans and cripples and maintaining maternity centres and child welfare clinics,

(xviii) providing facilities for anti-rabies treatment and meeting the expenses of indigent person undergoing anti-rabies treatment,

(xix) establishing rescue houses,

(xx) any other matter to promote education or the public health safety or convenience or the advancement of economic condition of the inhabitants.

Special Duties

Every municipality has to make reasonable provision for the following:

(i) providing special medical aid and accommodation for the sick in times of dangerous disease;

(ii) taking measures to prevent the outbreak or suppress and prevent the recurrence of the disease;

(iii) giving relief and establishing and maintaining relief works in time of famine or scarcity to or for destitute persons within the limits of the municipality.

Executive Officer

Every Nagar Panchayat or Council has an Executive Officer, who also functions as Secretary. All other officers and employees are subordinate to him. A Nagar Panchayat or Council appoints an Executive Officer with the concurrence of the State Government. If any Nagar Panchayat or Council does not make any such appointment, the State Government may make the appointment. A Nagar Panchayat or Council may, in addition to the Executive Officer, also appoint other officers to assist the Executive Officer with the concurrence of the State Government.

The Executive Officer works under the control of the Chairperson. He watches over the financial and executive administration of the Nagar Panchayat or Council and performs all the duties and exercises all the powers imposed or conferred upon him or delegated to him. The Executive Officer gives effect to the decision taken by the Nagar Panchayat or Council and submits periodical reports.

Other Officers and Staff

Every Nagar Panchayat or Council has a Health Officer, a Revenue Officer and an Engineer for the efficient discharge of its functions and duties.

A Nagar Panchayat or Council has power to appoint its officers and employees. The Chairperson may fill up non-technical posts on the Grade III and IV.

An employee who is aggrieved by an order of the Chairperson in disciplinary proceedings against him, has right to appeal to the Nagar Panchayat or the Council within 30 days from the date of service of such order on him. An employee who is aggrieved by an order of the Nagar Panchayat or the Council may prefer an appeal to the State Government against such an order within 60 days from the date of service of such order. However, no appeal against an order other than an order for removal or dismissal lies to the State Government. No disciplinary action, however, can be taken against the Executive Officer except with the approval of the State Government.

Conduct of Business

At least one meeting of the Nagar Panchayat or the Council for transaction of its business is held every month. If there is no business to be laid before any meeting, the Chairperson instead of calling the meeting, gives notice of the fact to each Councillor three days before the date of meeting.

The Chairperson, and in his absence the Vice-Chairperson may, on a written requisition of not less than one-half of the total number of Councillors, call a special meeting. If the Chairperson or the Vice-Chairperson fails to call a special meeting within 15 days of the requisition, the meeting may be called by the Councillors who made the requisition.

The Chairperson, or in his absence the Vice-Chairperson, presides over the meeting. In case of absence of both, the councillors present elect one of them to preside over the meeting.

All questions are decided by a majority of votes of the Councillors present and voting. In case of equality of votes, the person presiding has a casting vote.

No business can be transacted at a meeting unless a quorum of one-third of the total number of Councillors are present. If there is no quorum present, the Chairperson or the Vice-Chairperson can adjourn the meeting. A notice of adjournment is fixed upon the notice board in the municipal office. At the adjourned meeting any matter may be disposed of whether there is a quorum present or not.

Minutes of the proceedings of each meeting of the Nagar Panchayat or of a Council or its committee are recorded in a book kept for the purpose and are signed by the person who presides over the meeting. The minutes of the meeting are open to inspection, at all reasonable times and without charge by any member of the public. The minutes of the proceedings of all meetings are forwarded by the Executive Officer to the Deputy Commissioner, the Director and to the State Government.

No resolution can be modified or cancelled by a resolution supported by not less than two-thirds of the total number of

Councillors. Such resolution can be passed at a meeting whereof notice is given setting forth fully the proposed resolution to modify or cancel at such meeting and the motion of proposition for modification or cancellation of such resolution.

The Deputy Commissioner, the Director and such other officers specified by the State Government are entitled to attend any meeting to address it on any matter affecting the work of their department and to take part in the meeting, but have no right to vote.

Committees

The Nagar Panchayat or the Council may appoint committees to be called 'Standing Committee' to assist it in the discharge of any specific duties devolved upon it. Each committee consists of Councillors and residents with special qualification, appointed by the Nagar Panchayat or the Council at a meeting. In such meeting the number of Councillors should not be less than two-thirds of the total number of members of the committee. A councillor cannot be appointed at more than one committee at a time.

All the proceedings of any committee are subject to confirmation by the Nagar Panchayat or the Council at a meeting. All questions connected with the removal or resignation of members of the committee are settled by the Nagar Panchayat and the Council at a meeting.

The Chairperson of the Nagar Panchayat or of the Council is the ex-officio Chairperson of the Committee if he is a member thereof. In case the Vice-Chairperson is appointed as member, and Chairperson is not, he will be ex-officio Chairperson. In case both are not at the committee, the Chairperson of the committee is nominated by the Chairperson of the Nagar Panchayat or of the Council.

Municipal Taxation

The municipality may, with the prior approval of the State Government, impose in the whole or in any part, any of the following taxes and tolls:

(i) a tax on holdings assessed on their annual value, payable by the owner of the building or land or both,

(ii) a tax on vehicles or animals used for riding, driving, draught or burden and used within the municipal area;

(iii) an octroi on goods brought for sale, consumption or use;

(iv) a latrine tax payable by the owner or occupier for collection, removal and disposal of excrement or offensive matter from latrines, privies, animals, cesspools or compounds;

(v) a scavenging tax;

(vi) lighting tax where the lighting arrangement is made;

(vii) a drainage tax where a system of drainage has been introduced;

(viii) a tax on deeds of transfer of immoveable property;

(ix) a tax on advertisements;

(x) a water tax where water is supplied;

(xi) market fees on persons exposing goods for sale in any market or any place belonging to or under the control of the State Government or of the municipality;

(xii) a betterment charge on properties the value of which may be increased as a result of town planning schemes implemented by the municipality;

(xiii) any other tax, toll, rate, charge or fee.

Imposition of Tax

The State Government may direct the municipality to impose any tax or to modify the rate of any tax. On default of the municipality to comply with the decision within three months, the municipality is required to furnish its reason.

Assessment and Valuation

In order to prepare the valuation list, the assessor, by notice, requires the owners or occupiers of all holdings to furnish within fifteen days with returns of the rent or annual value and description of the holdings. A person failing to furnish the details or knowingly furnishing wrong details can be punished with fine not exceeding Rs. 500 and with further fine not exceeding Rs. 50 for each day during which he omits to furnish a true and correct return. A person obstructing, hindering or preventing the assessor appointed by the municipality from entering or inspection or measuring any holding can be punished with fine not exceeding Rs. 2000.

Annual value in case of hotels, schools, hospitals, factories and such other buildings, a proportion not exceeding five per cent of the sum obtained by adding the estimated present cost of erecting the building, less depreciation in the rate to be fixed, is determined. And in case of other building or land, the gross annual rent for which such building or land is actually let or where the building or land is not let or in the opinion of the municipality is let for a sum less than its fair letting value might reasonably be expected to let.

The municipality for general valuation, may appoint an assessor who is neither an employee nor a Councillor on pay and establishment determined by it. Such an appointment is made with the concurrence of the State Government.

A person dissatisfied with the amount assessed for him or with the valuation or assessment or who disputes his occupation of any holding or his liability to be assessed may apply to the municipality to review the amount within one month from the date of publication of notice. All such applications are given to the assessor. Every application is heard and determined by a committee consisting of not more than five members. The Chairperson or the Vice-Chairperson is one of the members of such committee and the other members are appointed from among the Councillors. No application is heard and determined by the committee unless at least three members including Chairperson or the Vice-Chairperson are present. The decision of the committee is final.

Municipal Property

All public roads including the soil, the pavements, stones and other materials thereof; and all drains, bridges, trees, erections, materials, implements and other things provided for such roads; all public streams, channels, water courses, springs, tanks, reservoirs, cisterns, wells, aquaducts, conduits, tunnels, pipes, pumps and other water-works, whether laid, made or created at the cost of the Nagar Panchayat or of the Council and all bridges, buildings, engines, works, materials and things connected therewith or appertaining thereto and also any adjacent lands, not being private property appertaining to any public tanks, all public sewers and drains, and all works, materials and things appertaining thereto and other conservancy works; all sewage, rubbish and offensive matters collected by the Nagar Panchayat or by the Council from roads, latrines, sewers, cesspools and other places; all public lamps, lamp-posts and apparatus connected therewith or appertaining thereto, and all public gates, markets, slaughter houses and public buildings and all lands or any property transferred to the Nagar Panchayat or Council by gift, purchase or otherwise for local public purposes within the municipality vest in the Nagar Panchayat or the Council. All such properties are under its direction, management and control, unless the State Government otherwise directs by notification.

No Nagar Panchayat or the Council can transfer any immoveable property except in pursuance of a resolution passed at a meeting by majority of not less than two-thirds of its members and except when it is not required for local public purposes.

Contract

Every contract made by or on behalf of the Nagar Panchayat or the Council in respect of any sum exceeding Rs. 10,000 is sanctioned by the Nagar Panchayat or the Council at a meeting and should be in writing and signed by at least two Councillors one of whom shall be the Chairperson or the Vice-Chairperson and, in the absence of both, the Executive Officer. Every contract is sealed with common seal.

Municipal Fund

Every municipality has a Municipal Fund to which all sums received by or on behalf of the Nagar Panchayat or the Council, the balance standing at the credit of the Nagar Panchayat or the Council, all proceeds of the disposal of property, all moneys raised by any tax levied for the purposes, all fees payable and levied, all moneys received by or on behalf of the municipality by way of compensation or for compounding offences, all moneys received from the State Government or private individuals by way of grants, contribution, gift or deposits, all interests and profit, arising from any investment of or from any transaction in connection with, any money belonging to the Nagar Panchayat or the Council.

Budget

A municipality at a meeting specially convened for the purpose, two months before the close of the financial year, prepares a budget showing the probable receipts and expenditure during the ensuing year and after revision, if any, it passes the budget. Such a budget is submitted to the Director for obtaining approval of the State Government. If the approval is not intimated within one month from the date of the receipt of the budget or the receipt of any information called for by the State Government, it is taken that the budget is approved.

The Nagar Panchayat or the Council may from time to time revise any estimates of expenditure and revised budget is passed in the like manner. Once the budget is passed the municipality cannot incur expenditure in excess of the sanctioned amount.

Accounts and Audit

Every municipality maintains accounts for every financial year and submits statement to the Deputy Commissioner, the Director and the State Government.

Accounts of the municipality are audited by the Director of Local Fund Audit and Accounts.

Rules and Bye-Laws

The State Government may by notification and with previous publication, make rules. Every rule made is laid before the Legislative Assembly.

A municipality may frame bye-laws consistent with the provisions of the Act and the rules made thereunder. The municipality situated in hilly tracts has additional power to frame bye-laws. No bye-laws can come into force until it is confirmed by the Government. The Government may cancel its confirmation of any bye-law. Every bye-law after confirmation is published in the prescribed manner.

Control

The Deputy Commissioner or the Director or any officer so empowered by the Government may enter into and inspect any immoveable property in the occupation or any work in progress under the control and maintenance of the municipality. He can call for inspection of any book or document in the possession or under the control of the municipality. The Government or the Deputy Commissioner may by order in writing suspend the execution of any resolution or order of the municipality or prohibit the doing of any act. When the Deputy Commissioner makes any such order, he forwards a copy thereof with a statement of his reasons for making it, to the Government. The Government may obtain the views of the Director and thereupon either rescind the order or modify it.

In case of any emergency, the Deputy Commissioner, upon the recommendation of the concerned technical adviser, is of the opinion that the immediate execution of any work or the immediate doing of any act is necessary for the health or safety of the public, he may call upon the municipality to execute the work within an appointed time. If such work is not executed within such period, he may appoint some other person to execute the work or do the act immediately. The Deputy Commissioner forthwith reports to the Government every case.

Dissolution

If, in the opinion of the Government, a municipality is not competent to perform or persistently makes default in the performance of the obligatory duties or exceeds or abuses its power, the Government may by notification stating the reasons declare such municipality to be incompetent or in default or to have exceeded or abused its power and dissolve it. The municipality is, however, given a reasonable opportunity of being heard before the dissolution.

Wards Committees

In respect of a municipality having population of three lakh or more, the State Government has to constitute Wards Committees. Each Wards Committee consists of not less than five wards. The geographical contiguity is maintained in constituting the Committees. Each Wards Committee consists of the members elected from the wards for which the Committee is constituted, and such other officers of the municipality as the State Government may specify to be ex-officio members, of whom one specified officer acts as the Secretary of the Wards Committee. The Executive Officer is the ex-officio member. The ex-officio members have the right to speak and participate in the meeting but cannot vote.

The Chairperson is elected by the members from among themselves.

The powers and functions of the Wards Committees and the manner of conducting business at its meeting are prescribed under rules.

District Planning Committee

The constitution of the District Planning Committee is provided in the Manipur Panchayati Raj Act, 1994. It consists of:

(a) members of the Lok Sabha who represent the whole or part of the district;

(b) all the members of the State Legislative Assembly whose constituencies lie within the district;

(c) Adhyaksha of the Zilla Parishad;

(d) Mayor or the President of the Municipal Corporation or the Municipal Council having jurisdiction over the headquarters of the District;

(e) such number of persons not less than four-fifths of the total number of members of the Committee from amongst the members of the Zilla Parishad, Nagar Panchayats and Councillors of the Municipal Corporation and the Municipal Councils in the district, in proportion to the ratio between the population of the rural areas and the urban areas in the district.

LIST OF TOWNS

Name of Town	*Population (1991)*	*Growth Rate (1971-81)*	*1981-91)*
1. Imphal	2,00,615	56.05	28.09
2. Churachandpur	33,657	138.50	62.09
3. Thoubal	32,730	226.79	76.27
4. Kakching	24,451	146.19	15.34
5. Mayang Imphal	16,529	-	125.74

(1)	*(2)*	*(3)*	*(4)*
6. Nambol	15,936	296.54	21.93
7. Samuraou	15,446	-	77.23
8. Moirang	15,417	52.85	20.39
9. Lilong	14,796	-	32.91
10. Thongkhong Laxmi Bazar	9,904	-	-
11. Morch	9.613	-	25.20
12. Lilong	9,420	-	37.06
13. Ningthonkhong	9,258	-	30.69
14. Kakching Khunon	8,237	-	-
15. Bishnupur	8,020	32.57	42.88
16. Lamjaotongba	7,338	-	-
17. Kumbi	7,252	-	14.60
18. Yairipok	6,887	-	52.60
19. Andro	6,796	-	-
20. Wangoi	6,749	-	(–) 6.37
21. Jiribam	5,946	-	35.38
22. Lamsang	5,632	-	23.32
23. Wangjing	5,619	-	20.58
24. Sikhong Sikmai	5,333	-	12.08
25. Oinam	5,305	-	8.87
26. Kwakta	5,030	-	-
27. Sekmai Bazar	4,406	-	9.38
28. Sugnu	3,997	-	(–) 8.30
29. Lamlai	3,605	33.35	21.83
30. Heirok	1,924	-	55.29

FOUR

Meghalaya

As earlier discussed, Meghalaya was a part of Assam State. The State of Meghalaya has three systems of local governance: modern municipal administration, Autonomous Hill District Councils and the native panchayat system. The State has adopted the Assam Municipal Act, 1956 for its urban governance. That is not being discussed here again. The chapter discusses in detail the system of local governance as practised in three autonomous hill districts.

UNITED KHASI-JAINTIA HILLS DISTRICT

The District Council of the United Khasi-Jaintia Hills Autonomous District enacted laws in 1961 to establish and develop local self government and to make better provision for administration of townships into well developed and self sufficient units. Towns in Meghalaya are those which have either been declared as such by the census or recognized as such by the District Council. The Executive Committee, with the previous approval of the District Council, can declare any town or area to be under the Town Committee. The area of the town under the jurisdiction of a Town Committee can be well defined after due enquiry is made by the officer of the District Council. The variation in area by the District Council cannot be made without first ascertaining the opinion of the representatives of the people.

Composition

A Town Committee can be formed on the representation of the elders of the town, and on due enquiry it can be ascertained that whether that town can form it. The elders are the prominent members of the localities who are nominated or elected by the people to look after their various affairs in the town. A Town Committee consists of not less than eight and not more than twelve representatives of the town whose membership is divided on the basis of adult suffrage. A certain percentage of the members can be nominated by the Executive Committee on the directions of the District Council.

The Town Committee can continue for a period of three years from the date of holding its first meeting after a general election. The period may be extended by the Executive Committee for a period not exceeding one year at a time.

Election

The election of the members may take place after giving due notice of not less than one month. The bye-election in case of death, resignation or removal of any member to fill the vacancy has to take place after due notice of one month. For the purpose of elections to Town Committee, the Executive Committee deputes any officer to enquire for the division of the area into 'dongs' (locality or part). Immediately after his report, the Executive Committee fixes the number of 'dongs' and the number of members to be elected to the Committee.

When the seat of an elected member falls vacant or the election of a member is declared void, the Executive Committee can direct a fresh election. If any person having been elected is found to be disqualified, the Executive Committee may, if the disqualification has not been removed, declare his seat vacant. In the event of any successful candidate being unwilling to serve as a member, within seven days from the declaration of the results, the Executive Committee may declare the unsuccessful candidate, who secured the next largest number of valid votes, to be duly elected.

If a person is elected to more than one seat, he has to resign all but one seat, within seven days. If he does not resign within the stipulated period of time, all the seats become vacant. In the event of any such vacancy arising in a 'dong', the Executive Committee can declare the candidate polling the next higher number of valid votes in that 'dong', as the duly elected member from that 'dong'.

Qualification of Members

A person is not qualified to be elected as a member and for being a member of Town Committee in the event,—

(i) if he is not a citizen of India or has voluntarily acquired the citizenship of a foreign state, or is under any acknowledgement of allegiance or adherence to a foreign state,

(ii) if he is of unsound mind and stands so declared by a competent court, or such other authority as may be recognized by the Executive Committee,

(iii) if he is an undischarged insolvent,

(iv) if, during the three years immediately preceding the date of the election, he has been convicted of an offence under the meaning of the Indian Penal Code, 1860,

(v) if, during the three years immediately preceding the date of the election, he has been convicted by a court for any offence and sentenced to transportation or imprisonment for not less than six months,

(vi) if, during the three years immediately preceding, he has been declared to be disqualified for employment in the public service,

(vii) if, during the three years immediately preceding, he has been debarred from practising as a legal practitioner by order of any competent authority,

(viii) if he is a salaried employee of the State or the Central Government, the District Council or of a Town Committee.

The disqualifications as referred in (iv), (v), (vi) and (vii) may be removed by the Executive Committee.

Chairman and Vice-Chairman

At the beginning of the new Town Committee or owing to the vacancy in the office of the Chairman, the Executive Committee fixes the date for holding of the election. An officer authorised by the Executive Committee presides over the meeting and conducts election. The election of the Vice-Chairman is conducted by the Chairman. The Chairman or the Vice-Chairman holds office for three years or the remainder of his term as member.

The Chairman exercises all the powers of the Town Committee. He cannot however exercise those powers without the sanction of the Executive Committee which are directed to be exercised by the Town Committee at a meeting.

Election Petition

A petition questioning the validity of the election of a successful candidate may be presented within thirty days from the declaration of the result to the Executive Committee. The Executive Committee refers the petition to the Commissioner appointed by it for the purpose. A sum of Rs. 50 is also deposited in the District Fund of the Council annually for the costs likely to be incurred and receipt thereof is submitted alongwith the petition. The Commissioner makes an enquiry and hears both the parties and if he is satisfied that substantial irregularity which materially affected the result or a corrupt practice has been committed, the election of the candidate becomes void. The Commissioner submits his report to the Executive Committee. In his report he also recommends as to the total amount of costs which are payable and the person by and to whom such costs should be paid and the manner of disposal of deposit of Rs. 50. For the purpose of enquiry, the Commissioner is empowered to summon witnesses, call for the production of any document and examine witnesses on oath or affirmation. On receipt of the Commissioner's report, the Executive Committee issues orders accordingly. In the event of the recommendation being made by the Commissioner that the election of the candidate should be held void, the Executive Committee sets aside the election and orders that a fresh election be held.

Conduct of Business

Ordinary meeting of the Committee is called by the Chairman at not less than 30 days interval, and special meetings may be called by the Chairman at shorter intervals. The Chairman or in his absence, the Vice-Chairman presides at every meeting and in the absence of both, the members choose one of them to preside over the particular meeting. All the proposals are decided by a majority of votes of the Committee. If the votes are equally divided, the Chairman has a casting vote. Every notice or bill may be served by presentation to the person to whom it is addressed or by serving it at his usual place of abode. The minutes of a meeting are recorded under the hand of the Chairman of the meeting. The quorum necessary for the transaction of business at a meeting including the Chairman and Vice-Chairman is three, where the total number of representatives is not less than eight but not more than nine, and five, when the total number of representatives are more than ten. In case of a meeting adjourned for want of quorum, a single member in addition to the Chairman or the Vice-Chairman forms the quorum.

Establishment

The Town Committee at a meeting may determine the establishment to be employed by it and may fix the salaries, allowances, pensions, gratuities and conditions of service of such staff. The appointment of any person on pay exceeding Rs. 50 per month has to be approved by the Executive Committee. The pay, allowances, etc., cannot exceed those admissible to the servants of the District Council.

Duties and Functions

The Town Committee may exercise all or any of the following functions:

(i) Maintenance of cleanliness and hygienic conditions of roads and paths, and prevention of public nuisance,
(ii) Maintenance of lighting installations,
(iii) Construction, maintenance and improvement of water supply,
(iv) Taking of curative and preventive measures in respect of epidemics,
(v) Opening and regulation of burial and cremation grounds for dead human beings and regulating places for disposal of refuse,
(vi) Maintenance of records relating to population census of employed persons, landless persons and any other statistics as may be required by the District Council,

(vii) Construction, maintenance and improvement of communication drains and waterways,

(viii) Control of grazing grounds, parks, beauty spots and other community property,

(ix) Relief of the poor, the sick or the victims of famine, flood or other calamity,

(x) Control and maintenance of public buildings, institutions and other properties belonging to or vested in the Committee or which may be transferred to their management,

(xi) Regulating the construction of new buildings or houses or the extension or alteration of existing ones,

(xii) Control and management of primary education,

(xiii) Enforcement of vaccination and other measures to combat and eradicate diseases and epidemics,

(xiv) Registration of birth and death and maintenance of registers for the purposes,

(xv) Prevention of epidemics in cattle,

(xvi) Promotion of maternity and child welfare,

(xvii) Supplying of local information as may be required by the District Council, State Government or any other authority through the Executive Committee,

(xviii) Planting and maintaining of trees at public places,

(xix) Construction and maintenance of Rest Houses,

(xx) Construction and maintenance of libraries, reading rooms, social and cultural clubs or other places of recreation and games,

(xxi) Promotion and popularization of modern sports and games that tend to promote the progress and welfare of people,

(xxii) Destruction of rabid and stray dogs and other dangerous animals,

(xxiii) Disposal of unclaimed cattle, horses, goats, buffaloes and other domestic animals,

(xxiv) Removal of encroachment on roads, public places and property vested in the Town Committee, and

(xxv) Any other function and powers as may be delegated by the District Council.

Power for Sanitary Purposes

The Town Committee may after issue of seven days' notice to the owner or occupier remove any encroachment upon any public property. A person who without the permission of the Town Committee encroaches upon any road, drain, sewer or water course is punishable with a fine not exceeding Rs. 50. The Committee may require any owner or occupier to trim or prune the hedges bordering on any road, to cut and remove any trees, bamboos or branches thereof, to eradicate any vegetation or to drain any land which is injurious to health or is offensive for want of drainage. If the owner or occupier fails to comply within a stipulated period of eight days, the Commissioner may carry out the work by its own agency and may recover the cost from the owner or occupier. The owner is liable for default in payment of the cost to a penalty not exceeding ten rupees for every day of default. Any person can not erect or re-erect a building without the sanction of the Town Committee. The Committee may require any building erected without permission to be demolished within one month and in case of default, it may get demolished by its own agency. A person committing such a breach is liable to a penalty not exceeding Rs. 50. The Town Committee has to seek the approval of the Executive Committee for erection of any building in Pyntharumkhash, Polo Hills, Goala Basti or areas deemed as beauty spots.

A person can not erect a latrine of a description other than such as may be approved by the Town Committee. Any person erecting in contravention is liable to a fine not exceeding Rs. 50. The Town Committee may require the owner or occupier to repair, make efficient, remove or fill up any latrine, urinal, cesspool, drain or receptacle for sewage or other offensive matters within a period of eight days. Any person failing to comply is liable to a penalty not exceeding five rupees for every day of default. The Committee has to provide for the removal and disposal of sewage, rubbish, and offensive matters and may require the occupier to deposit the same at such hours and places as it may fix. Any person flouting the schedule or allowing any rubbish, sewage or offensive matter to be kept upon such holding for more than twentyfour hours or allowing holding to be in a filthy or noxious state is liable for every such offence to a penalty not exceeding Rs. 50.

The Town Committee when required by the Executive Committee has to provide for the registration of births and deaths within its limit.

Water Supply

The Town Committee maintains by its own agency a water supply under its control and is responsible for the protection of the water works and for the supply of water within the area. It may set aside tanks, streams or wells for drinking, bathing or washing and may prohibit the use of any tank, stream or well for bathing or washing. Any person defiling the water supply or using any place for washing and bathing in contravention of a prohibition is liable to a fine not exceeding Rs. 50.

The Town Committee may execute any works necessary for the management of water supply subject to the payment of compensation for any damage done to private property. Any person interfering with the distribution of pipes without the sanction of the Committee or damaging the water supply is liable to a fine not exceeding Rs. 100. The Town Committee at a meeting may determine that a fixed quantity of water be supplied daily. It may grant private connections and may through any officer, enter upon private property for the inspection of the water installations. The Town Committee may cut off the supply of water of the person liable to pay water fee who neglects to pay or if he wilfully or negligently causes waste of water, and any person so causing waste is liable to fine not exceeding Rs. 20.

Sources of Revenue

The Town Committee has the power to levy and collect the following taxes:

(i) Taxes for the maintenance of primary schools established by it, and
(ii) Taxes for the maintenance of roads, bridges, paths and lanes constructed or maintained by it or which may be transferred to it for maintenance.

In addition, the Town Committee has power to impose and realize following fees:

(i) Fees for the use and for the maintenance of Rest Houses constructed by or transferred to the Committee,

(ii) Fees for the maintenance of public wells, tanks and water supply constructed by or transferred to it,

(iii) Fees for maintenance of lighting installation, and

(iv) Fees for conducting anti-epidemic services and other schemes of social services meant for the improvement of the public health and sanitation within the town.

Besides the above discussed tax sources, the District Council has to place at the disposal of the Town Committee the following sources of revenue accruing within its area:

(i) Cattle pound,

(ii) Local rates,

(iii) Carts, cycles, boats and other means of conveyance excluding mechanically propelled vehicles, and

(iv) Any other sources of revenue which may be assigned to the Committee by the District Council.

Tax Realization

The Town Committee has to frame rules for assessment and collection of taxes and fees. Collection of taxes and fees is made by authorised collectors of the Committee. The tax and fees are realized annually and they become due on the first day of each period fixed for the purpose. For the realization of arrears, the Committee can issue warrant for attachment and sale of any movable property belonging to the defaulter. The officer charged with the execution of warrant deposits the seized property in the office of the Committee for custody and gives ten days notice for the sale of seized property by beat of drums and by serving a notice upon the defaulter. If the demand is not paid within the period given in the notice, the seized property can be sold by public auction and the proceeds applied to the discharge of the arrears and costs. The surplus is paid on demand to the owner of the property.

Town Committee Fund

The District Council has to establish and maintain a Town Committee Fund to which have to be credited all contributions made from the District Council, Central and State Governments' contributions from Corporations, Societies, Companies or other public bodies and from other sources. All moneys received by the Committee in the course of the administration of town are credited to the fund. The Executive Committee may frame rules for the management and control of the fund. The fund can be utilized by the Town Committee to meet the charges in connection with the administration of the town.

The Town Committee Fund is maintained either in the Government Treasury or in the Post Office. Money may be withdrawn only by cheque or requisition on the Post Office signed by the Chairman. For meeting petty payments, a sum of Rs. 50 is given as permanent advance to the Chairman. All payments of less than ten rupees are made out of this advance. All orders for payments of money up to Rs. 500 are signed by the Chairman and orders for larger sums are signed by both the Chairman and Vice-Chairman.

Budget, Accounts and Audit

The Town Committee has to prepare annually a budget and submit it before the first day of February to the Executive Committee for consideration and approval.

The Town Committee may at any time during the year prepare a supplementary budget and submit it for the approval and sanction of the Executive Committee.

Any expenditure not provided for in a budget or supplementary budget may not be incurred without the specific sanction of the Executive Committee. The Chairman of the Committee may sanction re-appropriation within the budget up to Rs. 100 in any one case provided the closing balance sanctioned by the Executive Committee in the budget is not reduced. The Town Committee submits an annual report to the Executive Committee after the close of the financial year.

The Accounts of the Committee are audited as and when considered necessary by the Executive Committee. The audit is done by the Examiner, Local Accounts of the State Government. Audit reports are forwarded by the Examiner to the Chairman of the Town Committee and the Executive Committee. The Chairman is bound to remedy any defects or irregularities and within three months he has to submit a report giving particulars of actions taken to the Executive Committee, which forwards the same with its remarks to the Examiner.

Rules

The Executive Committee with the previous approval of the District Council may frame rules with regard to the delimitation of constituencies for the purpose of elections, qualifications for voting and the preparation of electoral rolls, qualifications for being elected as members, the term of office of members, procedure and the conduct of business, appointment of staff and any other matter related to or connected with the Committee for carrying out the administration. All rules framed by the Executive Committee have the force of law after publication in the Official Gazette of Meghalaya.

Control

The Executive Committee or any other officer employed by it has the power of inspection, supervision and control over the administration of the Town Committee in all its activities.

The Chief Executive Member or any officer of the District Council may enter upon or into and inspect any immoveable property in the occupation, or any work in progress, or any institution under the administration and control of the Committee. The Executive Committee, on its own motion, may by order in writing, suspend the execution of any resolution or order of the Town Committee or prohibit the doing of any act, if in its opinion, the same is likely to lead to a serious breach of the peace or to cause serious injury or annoyance to the public or to any class or body or person.

The Executive Committee may dissolve the Town Committee and take over its administration, if in its opinion, its continuance would adversely affect the peace, the welfare and the progress of the people of the town. If the Executive Committee feels that the Town Committee is not competent to perform or persistently makes default in the performance of its duties or exceeds or abuses its powers, the Executive Committee may, by notification stating the reasons for so doing, declare such Committee to be incompetent and supersede it for a period to be specified in the notification or dissolve and order for fresh election. In case of supersession, all the members have to vacate their offices, all the powers and duties of the Town Committee are performed by a person directed by the Executive Committee and all the property vested in the Committee vest in the Executive Committee. The Chairman, however, can normally perform all the functions and duties vested in the Chairman or Vice-Chairman.

Appeal

Any person aggrieved by an order of the Town Committee may appeal within thirty days of such order to the Executive Committee. The decision of the Executive Committee on the appeal is final.

JAINTIA HILLS AUTONOMOUS DISTRICT

A town in the Jaintia Hills Autonomous District means, any town or large village or area having a population of more than 8000 inhabitants, and notified by the Executive Committee in the Official Gazette of Meghalaya. The Executive Committee may, with the previous approval of the District Council, by notification in the Official Gazette, declare any town or area under a Town Committee. The area of a town under the jurisdiction of a Town Committee has to be well defined after due enquiry by an officer empowered by the Executive Committee. The District Council may however make changes in the area, after ascertaining the opinion of the Representatives of the people.

Constitution

A Town Committee can be established for any area on the representation of the elders of a particular area and when, after due enquiry it is found that such an area fulfills the prescribed conditions for establishing a Committee. The Executive Committee may constitute an ad-hoc Town Committee with nominated members not exceeding eight and for the period of not more than one year, which may be extended under special circumstances for a period of six months at a time but not exceeding a total life of three years.

Composition

A Town Committee consists of not less than eight and not more than twelve Representatives of a town whose membership is decided on the basis of adult suffrage. The Executive Committee may nominate a certain percentage of the members on the directions of the District Council.

Duration

The Town Committee, unless previously dissolved, can continue for a period of four years from the date of holding its first meeting after each general election. The period may be extended by the Executive Committee by a notification in the Official Gazette for a period not exceeding one year at a time.

Election

For the purpose of elections to Town Committee, the Executive Committee deputes any of its officers to enquire for the delimitation of the areas into 'Dongs' or Wards. Immediately after his report is submitted and after due consideration, the Executive Committee by a notification in the Official Gazette, fixes the number of 'Dongs' or 'Wards' and the number of members to be elected and nominated to the Committee. The Executive Committee by a notice published locally fixes the date for each election. In the case of a general election, the notice is issued not less than sixty days before the date fixed for the election and in the case of bye-election it is issued as soon as possible after the vacancy occurs, but at least forty five days before any such election. When the seat of an elected member falls vacant or the election of a member is declared void, the Executive Committee can direct fresh elections to be held to fill the vacancy.

If any person, having been found elected or nominated, is found to have been subject to any disqualifications, the Executive Committee may declare his seat vacant. In the event of any successful candidate being unwilling to serve by signifying in writing to that effect within seven days from the declaration of the result, the Executive Committee, if it is satisfied that the next unsuccessful candidate who secured a sufficient number of votes so as to command the confidence of the electorates of the ward, may declare him to be duly elected otherwise the seat can be filled up by holding a bye-election. If a person is elected to more than one seat in Town Committee, then unless within seven days from the date of publication of the result, such person resigns all but one of the seats, all the seats become vacant. If he resigns all but one seat, the remaining seats fall vacant.

Qualifications of Members

A person is disqualified from being elected as, and for being a member of a Town Committee:

(i) If he is not a citizen of India or has voluntarily acquired the citizenship of a foreign state, or is under any acknowledgement of allegiance or adherence to a foreign state,

(ii) If he is of unsound mind and stands so declared by a competent court, or such other authority as may be recognized by the Executive Committee,

(iii) If he is an undischarged insolvent,

(iv) If, during the three years immediately preceding the date of the elections, he has been convicted of an offence under the meaning of the Indian Penal Code, 1860,

(v) If, during the three years immediately preceding the elections, he has been convicted by a court of any offence and sentenced to transportation or imprisonment for not less than six months,

(vi) If, during the three years immediately preceding, he has been declared to be disqualified for employment in the public service,

(vii) If, during the three years immediately preceding, he has been debarred from practising as a legal practitioner by order of any competent authority;

(viii) If he is a salaried employee of the State, the Central Government or any autonomous body.

Election Petition

An election petition calling in question the validity of the election of a successful candidate may be presented within thirty days from the date of declaration of the result to the Executive

Committee. The Committee refers it to an Election Tribunal to be appointed by the Executive Committee for the purpose. A fee of Rs. 250 has to be deposited in the District Fund of the District Council as security for the cost likely to be incurred and the receipt thereof is submitted along with the petition. The Election Tribunal makes enquiries and hears both parties. If the Tribunal is satisfied that substantial irregularity which materially affected the result or a corrupt practice was committed, the election of the candidate becomes void. The Tribunal submits its report to the effect to the Executive Committee. In its report the Tribunal also recommends as to the total amount of costs which are payable and the person by and to whom such costs be paid. The Tribunal is empowered to summon witnesses, call for the production of any document, and examine witnesses on oath or affirmation. On receipt of the Tribunal's reports, the Executive Committee issues orders accordingly. In the event of the recommendations being made by the Tribunal that the election of the candidate should be held void, the Executive Committee can set aside the election and orders to hold a fresh election.

Chairman and Vice-Chairman

The Chairman and Vice-Chairman can hold office for four years. The Chairman can exercise all the powers of the Town Committee. He, however, can not act in contravention of any order of the Committee without the sanction of the Executive Committee.

Duties and Functions

A Town Committee may exercise all or any of the following functions:

(i) Maintenance of cleanliness and hygienic conditions of roads and paths, and prevention of public nuisance,

(ii) Maintenance of lighting installations,

(iii) Construction, maintenance and improvement of water supply,

(iv) Taking of curative and preventive measures to combat and eradicate diseases and epidemics,

(v) Opening and regulation of burial and cremation

grounds for dead bodies of human beings and regulating places for disposal of refuses,

(vi) Construction, maintenance and improvement of communication drains, grazing grounds, parks, beauty spots, rest houses, Town halls and other places of recreation,

(vii) Control, maintenance of public buildings and other properties belonging to or vested in the Committee or which may be transferred to their management,

(viii) Regulating the construction of new buildings or houses or extension or alteration of existing ones,

(ix) Registration of birth and death and maintenance of record for the purpose,

(x) Promotion of maternity and child welfare,

(xi) Supplying of local information and other statistics as may be required by the District Council, the State Government or any other authority through Executive Committee,

(xii) Destruction of rabid and stray dogs and other dangerous animals and disposal of unclaimed cattle, horses, goats, buffaloes and other domestic animals,

(xiii) Removal of encroachment on roads, public paths and properties vested in the Committee, and

(xiv) Any other functions and powers as may be delegated by the District Council.

Water Supply

The Town Committee may execute any work necessary for the management of the water supply in its area subject to the payment of compensation for any damage done to private property. Any person interfering with the distribution of pipes without the sanction of the Committee or damaging the water supply, is liable to a fine not exceeding Rs. 100. The Committee may determine the quantity of supply of water daily and in emergency according to the number of persons occupying each holding. The Town Committee at a meeting may grant private connection and may authorise any officer to enter upon private property for the inspection of the water installation. The Committee may cut off the supply of water of any holding if the person liable to pay the water tax neglects to pay or if he wilfully or negligently causes waste of water and is liable to a fine not exceeding fifty rupees.

The Committee may set aside tanks, streams or wells for drinking, bathing or washing and may prohibit washing. A person defiling the water supply or using any place for washing and bathing in contravention of prohibition, is liable to a fine not exceeding one hundred rupees.

Powers for Sanitary Purposes

A person who, without the permission of the Town Committee encroaches upon any road, drain, sewer or water course is punished with a fine not exceeding one hundred rupees. The Committee may, after issue of one week's notice to the owner or occupier of land, remove any encroachment upon any public property. The Committee may require any owner or occupier to trim or prune the hedges bordering on any road, to cut and remove any trees or bamboos or branches thereof which may appear to be in a state injurious to health or offensive for want of drainage. If the owner or occupier fails to comply within a period of eight days, the Committee may carry out the work by its own agency and may recover the cost from him. If the owner or occupier makes default in paying the cost, he is liable to a penalty not exceeding five rupees for every day of default.

A person can not erect or re-erect a building without the sanction of the Town Committee. The Committee may require any building erected without sanction to be demolished within a period of one month, and in default may demolish the building by its own agency. A person committing such a breach is liable to a penalty not exceeding two hundred rupees.

A person can not erect a latrine in any place and of any description other than an approved one by a competent officer appointed by the Town Committee. A person erecting in contravention, is liable to a fine not exceeding one hundred rupees. The Committee may require the owner or occupier to repair, make efficient, remove or fill up any latrine, urinal, cesspool, drain or receptacle for sewage or other offensive matter within a period not less than eight days. A person failing to comply is liable to a penalty not exceeding five rupees for every day of default. The Town Committee provides for the removal and disposal of sewage, rubbish and offensive matters and may require the occupiers of holdings to deposit the same at fixed hours and place. Any defaulter or a person allowing any rubbish, sewage or offensive matters to be kept for more than twentyfour hours or allowing a holding to be in filthy or noxious state is liable for every such offence to a penalty not exceeding one hundred rupees.

Power of Taxation

The Town Committee has the power to levy and collect house, water and latrine taxes and taxes for construction, maintenance and improvement of communication drains, and other places of public recreation within its jurisdiction. The Committee has also powers to impose and realise all or any of the following fees:

(i) Fees for the use and for the maintenance of Rest Houses constructed by or transferred to it,
(ii) Fees for the maintenance of public wells, tanks and water supply constructed by or transferred to it,
(iii) Fees for maintenance of street lighting, and
(iv) Fees for conducting anti-epidemic services and other schemes or social services for improvement of public health and sanitation within the town.

In addition, the Committee, with the approval of the District Council, has the power to impose and realize taxes on the following sources of revenue accruing within its area:

(a) Cattle pound,
(b) Local rates,
(c) Cart, cycle, and other means of conveyance excluding mechanically propelled vehicles,
(d) Any other sources of revenue which may be assigned to the Town Committee by the District Council.

The amount of tax or fee due from any person becomes due on the first day of each period fixed for the purpose. The Town Committee has to make rules for assessment and collection of taxes and fees. Collections are made by an authorised collector of the Committee. For the realization of arrear, the Committee can issue a warrant for attachment and sale of any moveable property belonging to the defaulter. The officer charged with the execution of warrant deposits the seized property in the office of the Committee for custody and has to give ten days notice for the sale of seized property by public announcement through loud speakers and by serving notice upon the defaulter. If the demand is not paid within the period, the seized property is sold by public auction and the proceeds applied to the discharge of the arrear and costs, the surplus is paid on demand to the owner of the property.

Staff

The Town Committee at meeting may determine the establishment to be employed by it and may fix the salaries, allowances, pensions, gratuities and conditions of service of such establishment. However, the appointment of any person on pay exceeding Rs. 200 per month has to be approved by the Executive Committee. The pay, allowances, pensions and gratuities to the employees of the Town Committee can not exceed those admissible to the District Council servants.

Conduct of Business

Ordinary meeting of the Town Committee can be called by the Chairman or in his absence by the Vice-Chairman at not less than 30 days interval. Special meetings may be called by the Chairman or the Vice-Chairman at shorter intervals. The Chairman or in his absence the Vice-Chairman presides at every meeting. In the absence of both, the members choose one among them to preside over the particular meeting.

The minutes of a meeting are recorded under the hand of the Chairman of the meeting. All the proposals are decided by a majority of votes of the Committee. If the votes are equally divided, the Chairman has a casting vote.

The quorum necessary for transaction of business is three when the total number of representatives is not less than eight but not more than nine and five, when the total number of representatives is more than ten. In case of a meeting having adjourned for want of quorum, a single member in addition to the Chairman or the Vice-Chairman forms the quorum.

Town Committee Fund

The District Council has to establish and maintain a Fund to be called a Town Committee Fund. Contributions from the District Council, from the State and Central Governments, from Corporations, Societies, Companies or other public bodies and all revenue receipts levied and collected by the Town Committee are credited to the Fund. The Fund can be utilized by the Town Committee to meet the charges in connection with the administration and other works connected with the town. The Town Fund vests in the Committee and may be kept in a Government Treasury or any Bank approved by the Executive Committee. The Committee sets apart and applies out of the Town Fund sums required to meet the charges of its establishment. It also provides for the maintenance and repair of all roads, bridges, tanks, wells, drains, and for the clearing of the area. It may apply the Town Fund under the approval of the Executive Committee to any matter as may be determined by the Executive Committee.

The Executive Committee may make rules for the management and control of the Town Fund. Such rules may prescribe the procedure, to be followed in respect of payment of money into this Fund, the withdrawal therefrom, its custody and any other matter connected with or ancillary to it.

Budget

The Town Committee has to prepare a budget of receipt and charges for each financial year. The estimates are submitted on or before the 2nd day of January to the Executive Committee for sanction. The Committee may at any time during the year, prepare a supplementary budget and submit it for the sanction of the Executive Committee. All expenditures provided for in a budget sanctioned by the Executive Committee may be incurred by the Committee.

An expenditure not provided for in a budget, may not be incurred by the Committee without specific sanction of the Executive Committee. The Chairman of the Committee may sanction re-appropriation within the budget upto Rs. 500 in any one case provided that the closing balance sanctioned by the Executive Committee in the budget is not reduced.

Accounts and Audit

The Town Committee has to maintain a classified cash book. A pass book is maintained for all moneys paid into or withdrawn from the Town Fund. All receipts are sent daily to the custodian of the Fund along with the Pass Book. All the withdrawals from the Town Fund have to be made by cheque signed by the Chairman or in his absence by the Vice-Chairman. For the purpose of meeting petty payments, a sum not exceeding Rs 250 is drawn once for all to be held as a permanent advance by the Chairman or the Vice-Chairman. All payments of less than ten rupees are made out of the permanent advance. All orders for the payment of money are signed by the Chairman or in his absence by the Vice-Chairman and for a sum not exceeding Rs. 500. The Chairman may delegate his powers to the Vice-Chairman. The Committee has to submit an annual report to the Executive Committee after the close of the financial year.

The accounts of the Committee are audited periodically by the Examiner of Local Accounts of the State Government. Copies of the audit reports are forwarded by the Examiner to the Chairman of the Town Committee and the Executive Committee. The Chairman is bound to remedy any defects or irregularities and within three months of the date of receipt of the audit report he has to submit a report giving particulars of the action taken to the Executive Committee which forwards the same with its remarks to the Examiner.

Rules

The Executive Committee may frame rules to carry out the administration in a town. The rules so framed can come into force immediately on publication in the Official Gazette of Meghalaya. The rules may provide for all or any of the matters including elections and by-elections, delimitation of 'Dong' or 'Ward', qualification for voting and the preparation of electoral rolls, qualifications for being elected as members, the term of office of the members, the procedure and conduct of the business, appointment of the staff and any other matter.

Control

The Chief Executive Member or any officer of the District Council authorised by the Executive Committee may enter upon or into and inspect any immoveable property in the occupation or any work in progress or any institution under the control and administration of the Committee. He may call for and inspect any book or document in the possession or under the control of the Committee.

The Executive Committee on its own motion may or on direction by the Governor through the Deputy Commissioner can suspend the execution of any resolution of the Committee or prohibit the doing of any act which is about to be done or is being done or in sanction or permission granted by the Committee, if in the opinion of the Executive Committee or of the Governor, it is in excess of the powers conferred or the execution of the resolution or order or the doing of acts is likely to lead to a serious breach of peace or to cause serious injury or annoyances to the pubic or to any class or body of persons.

Dissolution

If, in the opinion of the Executive Committee, the Town Committee is not competent to perform or persistently makes default in the performance of duties or exceeds or abuses its powers, the Executive Committee may declare the Committee incompetent or in default or to have exceeded or abused its powers and supersede it for a period to be specified in the notification or dissolve it and order for fresh elections. In case of supersession, all the members vacate their offices, all the powers and duties of the Committee are exercised and performed by persons as directed by the Executive Committee, and all property vested in the Committee vest in the Executive Committee. The Executive Committee has to report to the Governor any such action taken by it. The Chairman can however, normally perform all the functions and duties vested in the Chairman or Vice-Chairman.

Appeal

A person aggrieved by an order of the Town Committee may appeal, within thirty days of such order to the Executive Committee. The decision of the Executive Committee is final.

GARO HILLS AUTONOMOUS DISTRICT

The Executive Committee of the District Council may by notification published in the Official Gazette signify its intention to constitute a Town Committee for any specified area wherein it considers improved arrangements are necessary to deal with certain important local functions.

Composition

Each Town Committee consists of six members of whom four are elected and two nominated. In case the District Council so directs, all the members of a particular Committee may be appointed by the District Council for a specified period. The nominated members are appointed, by the Executive Committee and a member so appointed holds office during the pleasure of the District Council. The District Council, by notification, may increase the number of both the elected and nominated members of a particular Town Committee.

Duration

The Town Committee can continue for a period of three years from the date of holding its first meeting after the general elections. The period may be extended by the District Council by notification in the Official Gazette for a period not exceeding one year at a time. When the District Council has directed that all the members have to be appointed, they can hold office for the period specified in the directives.

Elections

For the purpose of elections to a Town Committee, the District Council can by notification in the Official Gazette divide the area into two or more wards and fix the number of members to be elected from each ward. The District Council by a notice published locally fixes the date for each elections. In the case of a general election, a notice is issued not less than sixty days before the date fixed for elections and in case of by-elections, a notice is issued as soon as possible after the vacancy occurs, but at least forty days before the by-election. When the seat of an elected member falls vacant or the election of a member is declared void, the District Council can direct fresh elections. If any person having been elected or nominated is found to have been subject to disqualifications, the District Council may, if the disqualifications have not been removed, declare his seat to be vacant. In the event of any successful candidate being found to be disqualified or unwilling to serve, within one week from the declaration of the result, the District Council may declare the unsuccessful candidate who secured the next largest number of valid votes, to be duly elected.

If a person is elected to more than one seat in a Town Committee, then unless within seven days from the date of his election, such person resigns all but one of the seats, all the seats become vacant. If he resigns all but one, the remaining seats become vacant. In event of such vacancy, the District Council can declare the candidate polling the highest number of valid votes in that ward, as the duly elected member from that ward.

Qualifications of Members

A person is disqualified for being elected and for being a member of a Town Committee:

(i) If he is not a citizen of India or has voluntarily acquired citizenship of a foreign State, or is under acknowledgement of allegiance or adherence to a foreign state;

(ii) If he is of unsound mind and stands so declared by a competent court or such other authority as may be recognized by the District Council;

(iii) If he is an undischarged insolvent;

(iv) If, during the three years immediately preceding the date of elections, he has been convicted of an offence under the Indian Penal Code, 1860;

(v) If, during the three years immediately preceding the date of elections, he has been convicted by a court of any offence and sentenced to transportation or imprisonment for not less than six months;

(vi) If, during the three years immediately preceding the date of elections, he has been declared to be disqualified for employment in public service;

(vii) If, during the three years immediately preceding the elections, he has been debarred from practising as a legal practitioner by order of any competent authority;

(viii) If he is a salaried employee of the State or Central Governments or of the District Council or is an employee of a Town Committee.

The disqualifications as referred in (iv), (v), (vi) and (vii) may be removed by an order of the District Council. The District council can nominate salaried person to be a member of the Committee.

Chairman and Vice-Chairman

At the first meeting of the Town Committee the members elect a Vice-Chairman from amongst themselves, and if authorised by the District Council to elect a Chairman as well, have to proceed to elect one of themselves as Chairman. In the event of the Committee being unable to elect a Chairman, it has to report the matter to the District Council. A Chairman or Vice-Chairman can hold office for three years.

The Chairman can exercise all the powers of a Town Committee. He, however, can not act in contravention of the Committee without the sanction of the District Council.

Election Petition

The validity of the election of any successful candidate can be questioned by presenting an election petition within one week from the date of declaration of the results to the Commissioner appointed for the purpose by the District Council. A sum of Rs. 25 has to be deposited in the District Fund as security for the cost likely to be incurred and receipt thereof submitted along with the petition. The Commissioner makes an inquiry and after hearing both the parties if he is satisfied that substantial irregularities which materially affected the result or a corrupt practice has been committed, the election of the candidate becomes void. The Commissioner submits his report to this effect to the District Council. In his report he has also to recommend as to the total amount of costs which are payable and the person by and to whom such costs should be paid and manner of disposal of deposit of Rs. 25. For the purpose of enquiry, the Commissioner is empowered to summon witnesses, call for the production of any documents and examine witnesses on oath or affirmation. On receipt of the Commissioner's report, The District Council issues orders accordingly. In the event of the recommendation being made that the election of the candidate should be void, the District Council sets aside the election and either may declare the candidate who secured the next largest number of valid votes to be elected or may order that a fresh election be held.

Conduct of Business

Ordinary meetings of the Committee are called by the Chairman at not less than 30 days interval. Special meetings may be called by the Chairman at shorter intervals if he considers the meeting necessary. All the proposals are decided by a majority of votes of the Committee. In case of equality of votes, the Chairman has a casting vote. The Chairman or in his absence the Vice-Chairman presides over the meeting. In absence of both, the members choose some one of them to preside over the particular meeting. The minutes of a meeting of the Committee are recorded under the hand of the President of the meeting. The quorum necessary for the transaction of business is three members including the Chairman or Vice-Chairman. In case of meeting adjourned for want of quorum, the quorum is a single member in addition to the Chairman or Vice-Chairman.

Taxation

The Town Committee may impose following taxes within the area under its jurisdiction:

(i) a general tax, payable by the owner, on holdings,

(ii) a water tax, payable by the occupier, on the annual value of the holdings,

(iii) a latrine tax, payable by the occupier, on the annual value of the holdings.

In addition, the Committee may charge rents, tolls and fees for the right to expose goods for sale in market under its control, and for the use of shops, stalls and standing therein.

Assessment and Valuation

The Committee at a meeting has to determine the valuation of all holdings after making necessary enquiries and to cause to prepare a valuation list. The list is revised every five year or earlier if the District Council so directs. The list is available to the inspection by tax payers at the office of the Committee. The annual value of holding is deemed to be seven and one-half per cent or any other rate as may be fixed by the District Council of the cost of erection of buildings. Where the cost of erection is not ascertainable, the gross annual rent at which holding may reasonably be-expected to be let is deemed to be the annual value. Before the close of the financial year, the Committee at a meeting determines the percentage on the annual value to be taken for the tax on holding. This percentage is applicable from the beginning of the next financial year.

After the percentage is fixed, an assessment register is prepared. It contains the number of the holdings, the annual value, the names of the owner and occupier, the amount of the tax on holding, the water tax and the latrine tax, the amount of the quarterly instalment and the reference of exemption.

The Committee presents a bill for the amount due to the person liable. If the amount is not paid within one month, the Committee may issue a warrant for the realization of the arrear by attachment and sale of any moveable property belonging to the defaulter. The officer charged with the execution of the warrant is responsible for the custody of the seized property and gives ten days notice of the sale by beat of drum and by serving a notice upon the defaulter. If the demand is not paid within the stipulated period, the seized property is sold in public auction and the proceeds are applied to the discharge of the arrear and costs. The surplus is paid on demand to the owner of the property.

Power for Sanitary Purposes

A person who encroaches upon the roads, drains, sewer or water course without the permission of the Town Committee, is punished with fine not exceeding Rs. 50. The Committee, may after giving notice of one week to the owner or occupier of any land, remove any encroachment upon any public property. The

Committee may require any owner or occupier to trim the hedges bordering of any road, to cut and remove any tree or bamboos, to eradicate any vegetation which may appear to it injurious to health or offensive, or to drain any land which may appear to be in a state injurious to health or offensive for want of drainage. If the owner or occupier fails to comply within eight days, the Committee may carry out the work and may recover the cost. In case of default in payment of the cost, the owner or occupier is liable to penalty not exceeding Rs. 10 for every day during the default.

A person can not erect or re-erect a building without the sanction of the Town Committee. The Committee may require any building erected without its permission to be demolished within a period of one month, and in default may demolish by its own agency. A person committing the breach is liable to a penalty not exceeding Rs. 50.

A person can not erect a latrine of a description other than an approved one by the Committee. Any one constructing in contravention is liable to a fine not exceeding Rs. 50. The Committee may require the owner or occupier to repair, make efficient, remove or fill up any latrine, urinal, cesspool, drain or receptacle for sewage or other offensive matter within eight days. Any one failing to comply is liable to a penalty apparently not exceeding five rupees for every day of default. The Committee can provide for the removal and disposal of sewage, rubbish and offensive matters. It may require the occupier to deposit the same at such hours and places as it may fix. Any person not following it or allowing any rubbish, sewage or offensive matters to be kept for more than twentyfour hours or allowing any holding to be in a filthy or noxious state is liable for every such offence to penalty not exceeding Rs. 50.

Water Supply

The Town Committee may execute any works necessary for the management of water supply. A person interfering with the distribution of pipes without the sanction of the Committee or damaging the water supply is liable to a fine not exceeding Rs. 100. The Committee may determine a fixed quantity of water to be supplied daily per rupee of tax or in case of emergency, according to the number of persons occupying the holding. The Committee may grant private connections to water supply and may depute any officer to enter upon private property for the inspection of the water installation. The Committee may cut off the supply of water tax to a holding if the person liable to pay the water tax neglects to pay the same or if he wilfully or negligently causes waste of water he is liable to a fine not exceeding Rs. 20.

The Town Committee may set aside tanks, streams or wells for drinking, bathing or washing and may prohibit the use of any tank, stream or well for bathing or washing. A person defiling the water supply or using any place for washing and bathing in contravention of a prohibition is liable to a fine not exceeding Rs. 50.

Town Fund

For every Town Committee a fund, to be called the Town Fund, is formed. All moneys received by the Committee are credited to it. The Fund is vested in the Town Committee and may be kept in a Government Treasury or in the Post Office Savings Bank. The Fund is used for the maintenance and repair of all roads, bridges, tanks, wells, drains, latrines, urinals and water supplies and for the clearing of the area. It may be applied for any other purpose subject to the control of the District Council. All receipts of the Town Fund are sent daily to the custodian of the Fund along with the Pass Book.

Accounts

The Town Committee maintains a classified cash book in which each item of revenue and the amount of each cheque drawn are recorded. Money may be withdrawn from the Town Fund only by cheque signed by the Chairman or, in his absence, by the Vice-Chairman or by both. No cheque is drawn for less than Rs. 10. For the purpose of meeting petty payments, a sum not exceeding Rs. 50, is drawn from the Fund as a permanent advance by the Chairman or the Vice-Chairman. All payments of less than Rs. 10 are made out of the permanent advance and are recorded in a separate register. All orders for the payment of money from the

Town Fund up to Rs. 500 are signed by the Chairman or Vice-Chairman, and all other orders by both.

Audit

The accounts of the Town Committee are audited periodically by the Examiner Local Accounts of the State Government. Copies of the audit reports are forwarded by the Examiner to the Chairman of the Town Committee and the District Council. The Chairman is bound to remove any defects or irregularities pointed out by the Examiner and within three months of the receipt of the audit report, he has to submit a report giving particulars of action taken to the District Council which forwards the same with his remarks to the Examiner.

Budget

The Town Committee has to prepare a budget of receipts and charges for each financial year and submit it on or before the 1st of March to the District Council for sanction. The Committee may prepare a supplementary budget and submit it on or before 1st March to the District Council for sanction. All expenditure provided for in the budget or supplementary budget sanctioned by the District Council, may be incurred by the Committee. No expenditure not provided for in a budget may be incurred by the Town Committee without the specific sanction of the District Council. The Chairman of the Committee may sanction to reappropriation within budget up to Rs. 100 provided that the closing balance sanctioned by the District Council in the budget is not reduced.

Staff

The Town Committee at a meeting may determine the establishment to be employed by it and may fix the salaries, allowances, pension, gratuities and conditions of service of establishment. The appointment of any person on pay exceeding Rs. 50 per month has to be approved by the District Council. The pay and all allowances and pensions and gratuities can not exceed those admissible to District Council servants of a like standing.

Control

The Chief Executive Member or any officer of the District Council authorised by the Executive Committee may enter upon or into and inspect any immovable property in the occupation or any work in progress under the orders or any institution under the control and administration of the Town Committee. The Executive Committee of the District Council, on its own motion, may or on direction by the Governor through the Deputy Commissioner, suspend the execution of any resolution or order of the Town Committee or prohibit the doing of any act which is in excess of the powers, or the execution of the resolution or order or the doing of act is likely to lead to a serious breach of peace or to cause serious injury or annoyance to the public, or to any class or body or persons.

Dissolution

If, in the opinion of the District Council, the Town Committee is not competent to perform or persistently makes default in the performance of the duties or exceeds or abuses its powers, the District Council may, by notification stating the reasons for doing so, declare the Committee to be incompetent or in default or to have exceeded or abused its powers and supersede it for a specified period or dissolve the Committee and order fresh elections. When an order of supersession is passed, all the members of the Committee vacate their offices, all the powers and duties of the Committee are exercised and performed by persons directed by the District Council and all property vested in it vest in the District Council. The Chairman can, however, normally perform all the functions and duties vested in the Chairman or Vice-Chairman. The District Council has to report to the Governor the action taken and the consequential arrangements made.

Appeal

Any person aggrieved by an order of the Town Committee may appeal within thirty days of such order to the District Council. The decision of the District Council on the appeal is final.

LIST OF TOWNS

Name of Town	*Population (1991)*	*Growth Rate (1971-81)*	*Growth Rate 1981-91)*
1. Shillong	2,22,273	42.32	27.23
2. Tura	45,677	127.63	29.55
3. Jewai	20,731	44.73	60.28
4. Nongartoin	14,378	-	270.57
5. Williamnagar	11,985	-	179.37
6. Cherapunjee	7,833	-	28.47
7. Baghmara	6,220	-	48.70
8. Shillong Cantonment			
9. Mawlai			
10. Nongthymmai			
11. Pynthor Umkhrah			
12. Madansting			

FIVE

Sikkim

Constitution of Municipality

The Governor may by notification declare any local area to be a Municipal area. The State Government has to, as soon as may be, but not later than ninety days from the date of declaration of a local area as a Municipal area, require to constitute in every such area a Municipality. Every Municipality is a body corporate having perpetual succession and a common seal with power to acquire, hold and dispose of property and to enter into contract. It can sue and be sued. However, in case of acquisition of disposal of immovable property, the Municipality has to obtain previous approval of the State Government.

Composition

A Municipality consists of :

(i) directly elected members not less than three and not more than nine,

(ii) the members of both the Houses of Parliament and the members of the State Legislative Assembly representing the constituency comprising wholly or partly the Municipal area, and

(iii) one member having special knowledge or experience in Municipal administration to be nominated by the State Government.

The members to be elected directly are chosen by direct election from the territorial constituencies in the Municipal area through secret ballot by persons whose names are included in the electoral,roll of the State Legislative Assembly for the time being in force. The nominated member has no right to vote in the meetings of the Municipality.

Reservation

The seats in every Municipality are reserved for the Scheduled Castes and the Scheduled Tribes. The number of seats so reserved bear the same proportion to the total number of seats to be filled by direct election as the population of the Scheduled Castes or the Scheduled Tribes bears to the total population of that area. One-third of the seats so reserved are reserved for the women belonging to these classes. Onethird of the total number of seats to be filled directly are reserved for women.

Disqualifications for Membership

A person is disqualified for being chosen as, and for being, a member of a Municipality

(i) if he is so disqualified for the purpose of election to the Legislative Assembly, or

(ii) if he is a member of a Gram Panchayat or Zilla Parishad, or

(iii) if he holds any office of profit under any local authority or a Cooperative Society or a Government company or a Corporation owned or controlled by the Central or the State Government, or

(iv) if he has been dismissed from the service of a State Government or Central Government or a local authority or a Cooperative Society or a Government Company or a Corporation owned or controlled by the Central or a State Government for misconduct, or

(v) if he is an undischarged insolvent, or

(vi) if he is of unsound mind and stands so declared by a competent court, or

(vii) if he is suffering from a variety of leprosy which is infectious, or

(viii) if he is convicted of an election offence, or

(ix) if he is convicted by a court of an offence involving moral turpitude and sentenced to imprisonment for a term not exceeding six months, or

(x) if he has not paid any arrear of tax or rate or fee payable to the Municipality or a Gram Panchayat or a Zilla Panchayat or the State Government, or

(xi) if he has directly or indirectly by himself or by his partner or employer or an employee held any share or interest in any contract with, by or on behalf of the Municipality.

Chairman and Vice-Chairman

Every Municipality elects at its first meeting, one of its elected members to be Chairman and another as Vice-Chairman in the case of Municipal Council and Sabhapati and Up-Sabhapati in the case of Nagar Panchayat.

The powers and duties of the Chairperson are to :

(i) regulate the meetings of the municipality,

(ii) be responsible for the maintenance of record and registers of the municipality,

(iii) exercise supervision and control over the acts done and actions taken by the members and officers and employees placed at the disposal of the municipality,

(iv) operate jointly with the Executive Officer the fund of the Municipality including the authorization of payments and refunds,

(v) cause to issue receipts under his signature or signature of the Executive Officer for sums of money received by him for and on behalf of the municipality,

(vi) cause preparation of all statements and reports required,

(vii) exercise other powers, perform functions and discharge duties as the Municipality may, by general or special resolution, direct or as the State Government may, by order, specify.

The Vice-Chairperson performs the following powers and discharges the following duties

(i) in the absence of the Chairperson, preside over and regulate the meetings of the Municipality,

(ii) exercise powers and perform functions and discharge duties of the Chairperson from time to time delegated to him by order in writing,

(iii) during the absence of the Chairperson, exercise all the powers, perform all the functions and discharge all the duties of the Chairperson.

Resignation

A Chairperson or a Vice-Chairperson or a member of a Municipality may resign his office by notifying in writing his intention to the State Government. A person tendering his resignation may withdraw his resignation before it is accepted. When the resignation is accepted, the prescribed authority communicates it to the members of the Municipality within thirty days of acceptance.

Removal

A Chairperson or a Vice-Chairperson may be removed from office by resolution of the Municipality passed by the majority of the members of the Municipality present and voting at a meeting specially convened for the purpose. A notice of such meeting is given to the prescribed authority. In the event of removal of a Chairperson or a Vice-Chairperson or when a vacancy occurs in either office, the Municipality elects another one. The person so elected takes office forthwith and holds office for the unexpired term of office of his predecessor.

The Secretary may, after giving an opportunity to a member of a Municipality to show cause against the action proposed to be taken against him, by order, remove him from office if:

(i) after his election he is convicted by a criminal court of an offence involving moral turpitude and punishable with imprisonment for a period of more than six months, or

(ii) he was disqualified to be a member of the Municipality at the time of his election,

(iii) he incurred any of the disqualifications after his election as a member, or

(iv) he is absent from three consecutive meetings of the Municipality without the leave of the Municipality.

A member so removed by the Secretary may, within thirty days from the date of the order, appeal to the State Government.

After giving the appellant an opportunity of being heard, the State Government may modify, set aside or confirm the order. The order of the State Government is final.

Transaction of Business

The Secretary as soon as may be but not later than thirty days from the date of announcement of the result of the election, convene the first meeting of the Municipality. The members before taking their seats, make and subscribe before the Secretary an oath or affirmation. There is held at least one meeting of the Municipality in every three months on the date and time fixed by the Chairperson. The Chairperson and, in his absence, the Vice-Chairperson may, whenever he thinks fit, in the public interest and has to, on a written requisition of not less than one half of the total number of members, call a special meeting within a period of ten days from the date of receipt of the requisition.

The quorum is twothirds of the total number of members of the Municipality.

The Chairperson or , in his absence, the Vice-Chairperson presides over the meeting. In absence of both, the members present elect one member from amongst themselves to preside over the meeting.

All questions are decided by a majority of voters of the members present and voting. In case of equality of votes, the presiding person has a second vote.

A subject once finally disposed of by the Municipality can not be considered within six months unless the recorded consent of not less than one half of members has been obtained. A notice listing the business to be transacted at every meeting is sent to each member at least seven days before the time fixed for meeting. In case of an emergent meeting, the Chairperson may call the meeting after giving three days notice.

The minutes of the proceedings of each meeting are recorded in a book kept for the purpose. It is signed by the person who presided over the meeting. A copy of the minutes of all meetings are forwarded to the State Government by the Chairperson. The minutes, at all reasonable times and without charges, are kept open to inspection of the tax payers.

Any resolution cannot be modified or cancelled except by a resolution supported by not less than two thirds of the total number of members and passed at a meeting.

Executive Officer

In every Municipality an Executive Officer is appointed by the State Government. He functions as the Secretary to the Municipality and all other officers and employees are subordinate to him. The same officer may be appointed by the State Government to function as Executive Officer of two or more Municipalities.

The Executive Officer, subject to the general control of the Chairperson, watches over the financial and executive administration of the Municipality and performs all duties and exercises all the powers imposed or conferred upon him and gives effect to the decision taken by the Municipality and submits periodical reports regarding the progress to the State Government.

Municipal Establishment

A Municipality with the approval of the State Government, may appoint officers and employees to assist the Executive Officer. A Municipality may require the State Government to keep at its disposal the services of a Health Officer, a Revenue Officer and an Engineer.

The manner of appointment, conditions of service of the employees, powers and functions and disciplinary actions against the Executive Officer, other officers and employees are such as may be prescribed.An employee aggrieved by an order of the Chairperson may prefer an appeal to the Municipality against such order within thirty days from the date of service of such order. An employee aggrieved by an order of the Municipality has a right to prefer an appeal to the State Government within sixty days from the date of service of such an order. No appeal against an order other than an order for removal or dismissal can lie to the State Government.

Municipal Property

All property within the Municipality other than the private property or property maintained by the Government or other local authority vests in the Municipality. All public roads including soil, pavements, stones and other materials and all drains, bridges, trees, erection, materials, implements, all public streams, channels, water sources, springs, tanks, reservoirs, cisterns, wells, aquaducts, conduits, tunnels, pipes, pumps and other water works, all bridges, buildings, engines works, materials and things connected therewith, all public sewers and drains, and all works, materials and things appertaining thereto and other conservancy works, all sewage, rubbish and offensive matters collected from roads, latrines, sewers, cesspools and other places, all public lamps, lamp posts and apparatus connected therewith and all public gates, markets, slaughter houses and public buildings and all lands and other property transferred to the Municipality by the Government or acquired by the Municipality by gift, purchase or otherwise for local public purposes vests in the Municipality.

A Municipality cannot transfer any immovable property except in pursuance of a resolution passed at a meeting by a majority of not less than two-thirds of its members and except when it is not required for local public purposes.

Contracts

Every contract made by or on behalf of the Municipality in respect of any work exceeding Rs. 10,000 can be sanctioned by the Municipality at a meeting. It is made in writing. Every contract is signed by the Chairperson or the Vice-Chairperson and the Executive Officer and is sealed with the common seal of the Municipality.

Municipal Fund

Every Municipality has a fund called Municipal Fund. All sums received as grants-in-aid, all sums received by or, on behalf of the Municipality, the balance, all proceeds of the disposal of property, all rents accruing from any property, all moneys raised by any tax, all fees payable and levied, all moneys realized by way of compensation or for compounding offences, all moneys received from private individuals by way of grants, contribution, gift or deposits and all interest and profits arising from any investment of, or from any transaction in connection with any money belonging to the Municipality are credited to the Municipal Fund.

Budget

Every Municipality at a special meeting at least two months before the close of the financial year, prepares a budget showing interalia the probable receipts and expenditure during the ensuing year. The budget is submitted to the State Government for approval. If the approval is not intimated within one month, it is treated that the budget is passed.

Accounts and Audit

Every Municipality has to maintain proper records of all receipts and expenditure. As soon as may be after the 1st of April each year, the Municipality prepares a detailed report of the Municipal administration of the town during the previous year, together with a statement showing the accounts of the receipts and disbursements and the balance at the credit of the Municipal Fund at the close of the year. The Executive Officer places the report and statement before the meeting of the Municipality for consideration and forwards a copy to the State Government. The Executive Officer also prepares monthly abstract of the receipts and expenditure of the month last preceding and places before the meeting of the Municipality for consideration and approval.

An officer not below the rank of the Chief Accounts Officer audits the accounts of the Municipality as early as may be after the end of each financial year. The auditor may require the production of any document or the supply of any information may require the personal appearance of any person accountable for, or having the custody or control of any document or having any interest and may require any person to make or sign a declaration in respect of any document or to answer any question or prepare and submit any statement. Any person who neglects or refuses to comply with the requisition made by the auditor is, on conviction by a court, punishable with fine, which may extend to two hundred rupees in respect of each item included in the requisition. The auditor has to submit within two months from the date of audit, a report to the Chairperson and to the State Government. The Municipality within two months of the receipt of the report, at a meeting removes any defect or irregularity pointed out in the report and informs the auditor of the action taken. In case of failure of the Municipality, the auditor refers the matter to the State Government. On receipt of the report, the State Government is competent to pass any order. The orders of the State Government are final and the Municipality takes action accordingly. If the Municipality fails to comply with the order within the period specified, the State Government may empower any officer to carry out the order.

The auditor can make surcharge or charge of any person. An aggrieved person may, within thirty days of the receipt of the surcharge, appeal to the State Government to set aside or modify the disallowance, surcharge or charge and the State Government may pass orders, which are final.

Municipal Taxation

With the previous approval of the State Government, a Municipality may impose in the whole or part of it, any of the following taxes, fees and tolls:

(i) a tax on holdings situated within the Municipality, assessed on their annual value, payable by the owner of the building or land or both,
(ii) a tax on vehicles or animals used for riding, driving, drought or burden and used within the limits of the Municipality,
(iii) a latrine tax, payable by the owner or occupier for collection, removal and disposal of latrines, urinals, cesspools or compounds by the municipal agency,
(iv) an octroi on goods brought within the limits of the Municipality for sale, consumption or use,
(v) a lighting tax where the lighting arrangement is made by the Municipality,
(vi) a drainage tax,
(vii) a tax on deeds of transfer of immovable property situated within the limits of the Municipality,
(viii) a tax on advertisements,
(ix) a water tax,
(x) market fees on persons exposing goods for sale in any market or in any place belonging to or under the control of the State Government or of the Municipality,
(xi) a betterment charge on properties, the value of which may be increased as a result of town planning scheme implemented by the Municipality,
(xii) a tax on theatres, theatrical performance and other shows for public amusement,
(xiii) a duty on the transfer of property,

(xiv) a tax on professions, trades and callings,
(xv) a tax on dogs kept within the Municipal area,
(xvi) a toll on vehicles and animals entering the Municipal area but not liable under (ii),
(xvii) a tax on pilgrims resorting periodically to a shrine within the municipal limits,
(xviii) a tax on passengers and goods carried by road,
(xix) any other tax, toll, rate, charge or fee.

Annual Value

In the case of hotels, colleges, hospitals, factories and other such buildings, a proportion not exceeding five per cent by adding the estimated value of the land appurtenant thereto is the annual value. In the case of other lands and buildings, the annual value is the gross annual rent for which such buildings or land is actually let or where the building is not let or, in the opinion of the Municipality, is let for a sum less than its fair letting value, might reasonably be expected to let.

Recovery of Claims

If the tax payable by the owner of any holding remains unpaid after the notice of demand has been duly served and if such owner is not a resident within the Municipality or the place of abode of the owner is not known, the tax may be recovered from the occupier for the time being, who may deduct from the following payment of the rent.

The owner is empowered to recover from the amount the entire amount of the tax.

When any sum is due on account of a tax, other than octroi or toll or any similar tax payable upon immediate demand from a person to a Municipality, the Municipality may apply to the Certificate Officer, to recover such sum together with costs of proceedings incurred. The Certificate Officer can proceed to recover the amount as public demand.

If the owner of any holding or his whereabouts are unknown or the ownership is disputed or the owner lives outside the Municipality and has failed to pay in spite of service of demand notices twice, the Municipality may publish twice, at an interval of three months, a notification of sale of such holding and after the expiry of three months from the date of publication, may sell holding to the highest bidder. After deducting the amount due, the surplus proceeds are credited to the Municipal Fund and may be paid on demand or in a court of competent jurisdiction.

Functions

Every Municipality has to perform functions relating to :

(i) Urban planning including town planning,
(ii) Regulation of land use and construction of buildings,
(iii) Planning for economic and social development,
(iv) Roads and bridges,
(v) Water supply for domestic, industrial and commercial purposes,
(vi) Public health, sanitation, conservancy and solid waste management,
(vii) Fire services,
(viii) Urban forestry, protection of the environment and promotion of ecological aspects,
(ix) Safeguarding the interest of weaker section of society, including the handicapped and mentally retarded,
(x) Slum improvement and upgradation,
(xi) Urban poverty alleviation,
(xii) Provision of urban amenities and facilities such as parks, gardens, playgrounds,
(xiii) Promotion of cultural, educational and aesthetic aspects,
(xiv) Burials and burial grounds, cremations, cremation grounds, and electric crematoriums.
(xv) Cattle pounds, prevention of cruelty to animals,
(xvi) Vital statistics including registration of births and deaths,
(xvii) Public amenities including street lighting, parking lots, bus stops and public conveniences,
(xviiii) Regulation of slaughter houses and tanneries.

Fire Brigade

For the prevention and extinction of fire, the Municipality may resolve to establish and maintain a fire brigade and to provide any implements, machinery or means of communicating intelligence which the Municipality may think necessary for the efficient discharge of their duties by the brigade. The Municipality may recognize and aid a volunteer fire-brigade and provide for the guidance, training, discipline and conduct of the members thereof.

Election Petition

The election of a person as a member can be called in question by an application presented to prescribed authority within a fixed time.

No person can contest the election to any Municipality with the support of any political party.

Rules and Bye-Laws

The State Government may make rules for carrying out the purposes of the Act.

A Municipality may, with the previous approval of the State Government, frame bye-laws.

Control

The Secretary may enter into and inspect or cause any other person to enter into or inspect any immovable property in the occupation of or any work in progress under or any institution under the control and administration of the Municipality and call for and inspect any book or document which may be in the possession or under the control of the Municipality.

The State Government or the Secretary may suspend the execution of any resolution or order of the Municipality or prohibit the doing of any act if in its or his opinion, the resolution, order or act is contrary to the public interest or is in process of doing of the act, likely to lead to a serious injury or annoyance to the public, or to any class or body of persons. When the Secretary makes any such order, forthwith forwards a copy thereof, with a statement of his reasons for making it, to the State Government, which may rescind the order or direct that it continues to be in force, with or without modification permanently or for any period. However the concerned Municipality is given an opportunity of being heard against such proposed action.

On receipt of a complaint or information or otherwise, if it appears to the State Government that the Municipality has made default in performing any duty, the State Government may call upon the Municipality to perform the duty within a stipulated period of time. If such duty is not performed, the State Government may, after considering any representation of the Municipality, either revoke or modify the order or appoint some fit and proper person to perform the duty.

If, in case of emergency, the Secretary, upon the recommendation of the technical advisor, is of the opinion that the immediate execution of any work or the immediate doing of any act is necessary for the health or safety of the public, he may call upon the Municipality to execute the work within the appointed time. If such work is not executed within prescribed time, he may appoint some fit and proper person to execute the work or do the act immediately. The Secretary forthwith reports to the State Government every such case whereupon the State Government may pass appropriate orders.

Dissolution

If, in the opinion of the State Government, a Municipality is not competent to perform, or persistently makes default in the performance of the duties imposed upon it or exceeds or abuses its powers, the State Government may, by notification, stating the reason for so doing, declare such Municipality to be incompetent or in default or to have exceeded or abused its powers and supersede or suspend it for a period not exceeding two months at a time or direct the Municipality and order a fresh election within six months. The period of supersession and suspension cannot exceed a period of six months in total.

When an order of suspension, supersession or dissolution is passed, all the members vacate their offices, all the powers and duties are exercised and performed by such person as the State Government may appoint and all properties vested in the Municipality vest in the State Government.

District Planning Committee

The State Government has to constitute in every district a District Planning Committee. It consists of the member of the House of People, the member of Council of State, Adhyaksha of Zilla Panchayat, Chairperson of Municipalities having jurisdiction over the headquarters of the district and not less than four-fifth of the total number elected from amongst the elected members of Municipalities and Zilla Panchayat in the district in proportion to the ratio between the population of the rural areas and of the urban areas in the district. In addition, all the members of the Legislative Assembly whose constituencies lie within the district and who are electors in the district, the District Collector of the district and the District Development Officer-cum-Panchayat Officer are the permanent invitees of the Committee. The Adhyaksha of the Zilla Panchayat is the Chairman and the District Development Officer-cum-Panchayat Officer is the Member Secretary.

The District Planning Committee has to consolidate the plans prepared by the Zilla Panchayat, Gram Panchayats and Municipalities in the district and to prepare a draft development plan for the district as a whole.

State Finance Commission

The State Finance Commission constituted under the Constitution and the Sikkim Panchayat Act, 1993 is empowered to review the financial position of the Municipalities and make recommendations to the Government.

State Election Commission

The superintendence, direction and control of the preparation of electoral rolls for and the conduct of all elections to the Municipalities rests in the State Election Commission constituted by the Governor under the Sikkim Panchayat Act, 1993.

LIST OF TOWNS

Name of Town	*Population*	*Growth Rate*	
	(1991)	*(1971-81)*	*1981-91)*
1. Gangtok	24,971	176.13	(–) 32.05
2. Singtum	3,880	109.92	(–) 4.03
3. Rangpo	2,970	37.37	21.13
4. Jorethang	1,962	414.57	(–) 49.96
5. Naya Bazar	1,043	46.24	9.56
6. Mangan	803	135.65	2.95
7. Gyalshing	717	67.42	(–) 3.76
8. Namchi	638	213.91	(–) 55.82

SIX

Tripura

In pursuance of the Constitutions (74th Amendment) Act, 1992 and in view of the provisions of the Sixth Schedule of the Constitution, the State Legislative Assembly enacted the Tripura Municipal Act, 1994 to reorganize the Municipality in urban and town areas of Tripura and to provide for matters connected therewith and incidental thereto. It extends to the whole of the State of Tripura except the areas under the Tripura Tribal Areas Autonomous Districts.

Notification of Municipal Areas

The Governor declares an area as urban area when it:

(i) contains a population of not less than 5 lakhs as larger urban area or not less than 50,000 as smaller urban area or less than fifty thousand as transitional area,

(ii) has a density of not less than 500 per sq. km. of area,

(iii) has an occupational pattern in which more than one half of the adult population are chiefly engaged in pursuits other than agriculture, and

(iv) the revenue generated for local administration is likely to be adequate for discharge of municipal functions.

Constitution of Municipalities

The State Government can constitute:

(a) a Nagar Panchayat for transitional urban area, i.e., area having population less than 50,000;

(b) a Municipal Council for a smaller urban area i.e., area having a population more than 50,000 but less than 5 lakhs;

(c) a Municipal Corporation for a larger urban area having a population of 5 lakhs or more.

Composition of Municipalities

Each Municipality may consist of:

(i) *Elected Members*

(a) Municipal Corporation	:	not less than 20 and not more than 40;
(b) Municipal Council	:	not less than 5 and not more than 15;
(c) Nagar Panchayat	:	not less than five and not more than 15;

(ii) *Nominated Members*

The persons having special knowledge or experience in Municipal Administration are nominated by the Governor as under:

(a) Municipal Corporation	:	5,
(b) Municipal Council	:	3; and
(c) Nagar Panchayat	:	2;

(iii) *Ex-Officio Members*

The Chairpersons of the Wards Committees and other committees.

The nominated members do not have the right to vote in the meetings of the Municipality.

For the purpose of election, every Municipal area is divided into wards. Every ward forms a single member constituency. The seats are allotted on population of not less than eight hundred in larger or smaller urban areas and not less than such population as the State Government may determine for transitional areas.

Reservation of Seats

In pursuance of the Constitutional Amendment Act, the State Government provides for reservation of seats:

(i) for the Scheduled Castes and the Scheduled Tribes in ratio of proportion to their population to the total population,

(ii) not less than one-third of the total number of seats reserved for the women belonging to these classes;

(iii) not less than one-third of the seats are reserved for the women.

The seats of the Chairpersons are also reserved on the same pattern.

Standing Committees

Each Municipality may have the following Standing Committees:

(i) Finance Committee
(ii) Public Health Committee, and
(iii) Public Works Committee.

Each Standing Committee consists of the members elected by and from amongst the elected members -

(a) in the case of Municipal Corporation — 6,
(b) in the case of Municipal Council — 4, and
(c) in the case of Nagar Panchayat — 3.

In addition, the State Government may nominate not more than four members being officers of the State Government having requisite expertise for development of municipal services and their maintenance. The nominated members have no right to vote at a meeting of the Standing Committees.

The Chairperson of the Municipality is the ex-officio President of the Finance Committee. The Presidents of other Standing Committees are appointed by the Chairperson from amongst the members of such Committees. If the Vice-President of the Municipality is a member of the Committee, he shall be the ex-officio President of the Committee, if the Chairperson is not in the Committee.

The term of the office of a member of a Standing Committee is two and a half years. No members except the Chairperson can be member of more than two Standing Committees. A member may resign any time by writing under his hand and addressed to the Chairperson of the Municipality. The removal of a member can be done by rules made by the State Government.

The Municipal Secretary or such officer as may be appointed by the Chairperson shall be ex-officio Secretary of the Standing Committee.

The proceedings of every Standing Committee in the form of a report is presented to the Chairperson by the President or by any member of the Committee authorized by it and is subject to confirmation, modification or rejection by the Municipality. Each Standing Committee performs such functions, exercises such powers and discharges such duties as are prescribed or assigned to it by the Municipality.

Special Committee

The Municipality may appoint a Special Committee to perform specified functions or conduct enquiries or undertake studies including reports thereon. The number of members are contained in a resolution in this behalf. The manner of transaction of business is laid down by the Municipality.

Joint Committee

The State Government may constitute a Joint Committee for one Municipality or more Municipalities with other local authority or authorities for any purpose in which they are jointly interested or for delegating to it any power or function which calls for joint action.

The Joint Committee consists of two nominees of each constituent Municipality or local authority; one nominee of each of the concerned departments of the State Government; and such experts as the State Government may nominate. The procedure of transaction of business is prescribed by the State Government.

MUNICIPAL AUTHORITIES

The Municipal Authorities charged with the responsibilities are:

(i) in case of Municipal Corporation
  (a) the Municipal Corporation,
  (b) the Mayor-in Council,
  (c) the Mayor;

(ii) in case of Municipal Council
  (a) the Municipal Council,
  (b) the Chairperson-in-Council,
  (c) the Chairperson; and

(iii) in case of a Nagar Panchayat
  (a) the Nagar Panchayat,
  (b) the Chairperson-in-Nagar Committee,
  (c) the Chairperson.

Nagar Panchayat

It is the legislative body of the Municipality of transitional urban area. All the legislative actions are expressed to be made in the name of the Municipality.

Nagar Committee

It is an executive body consisting of the Chairperson, the Vice-Chairperson and other members not exceeding three. The Vice-Chairperson and members are nominated by the Chairperson from amongst the elected members of the Nagar Panchayat. All executive powers vest in the Chairperson-in-Nagar Committee. It is collectively responsible to the Nagar Panchayat. The manner of transaction of business is such as may be prescribed.

Chairperson

The Chairperson is the executive head and the administration is under his control. He allocates the business among the members of the Nagar Committee. The Chairperson presides over the meetings of the Nagar Committee as well as of the Nagar Panchayat. He can transact any business or make any order but not in opposition to or in contravention of any decision of the Nagar Panchayat.

The elected members of the Nagar Panchayat elect one of its members to be the Chairperson. In case the elected members fail to elect a Chairperson, the State Government can appoint by name one of such elected members. In case of any casual vacancy in the office, the elected members elect one of the members to fill up the vacancy.

The Chairperson ceases to hold office if he ceased to be a member of Nagar Panchayat. The Chairperson by giving a notice in writing to the Vice-Chairperson or if there is no Vice-Chairperson, to the Nagar Panchayat, resigns his office. The Chairperson may be removed from office by a resolution carried by a majority of the total number of elected members of the Nagar Panchayat at a special meeting called for the purpose. Such a meeting is called upon a requisition made in writing by not less than one-third of the total number of elected members of the Nagar Panchayat. However, no such resolution can be moved before the expiry of six months from the date of assumption of office by the Chairperson. In case of non-adoption of such a resolution no further resolution for such purpose can be moved before the expiry of a period of six months from the date on which the former resolution was moved.

The Chairperson of a Nagar Panchayat whose office becomes vacant continues to hold office as Chairperson until his successor enters upon his office.

Vice-Chairperson

The Vice-Chairperson, in the absence of the Chairperson, presides over the meetings of the Nagar Committee as well as of the Nagar Panchayat. He, in the absence of the Chairperson, discharges all duties and exercises all powers of the Chairperson unless otherwise expressly directed by the Chairperson. The Vice-Chairperson performs, such other duties or exercises such other powers as are delegated to him.

The Vice-Chairperson or the members of the Nagar Committee hold office until:

(a) he ceases to be a member of the Nagar Panchayat, or
(b) he resigns his office by writing under his hand addressed to the Chairperson. Such a resignation takes effect from the date of its acceptance, or
(c) he is removed from office by a written order of the Chairperson, or
(d) in the case of the death of the Chairperson, a newly elected Chairperson enters upon his office.

MUNICIPAL COUNCIL

The Municipal Council is the legislative body of the Municipality in smaller urban area.

Chairperson-in-Council

It is the executive body consisting of the Chairperson, the Vice-Chairperson and other members not exceeding five. The Vice-Chairperson and other members are nominated by the Chairperson from amongst the elected members. All executive powers vest in it. It is collectively responsible to the Municipal Council.

Chairperson

The elected members of the Municipal Council elect one of its members as the Chairperson. In case of their failure, the State Government appoints by name any of the elected members to be the Chairperson. In case of any casual vacancy, the elected members elect one of the elected members to fill up the vacancy.

The Chairperson is the executive head of the Municipality and the administration is under his control. He presides over the meetings of the Chairperson-in-Council as well as of the Municipal Council. He may transact any business or make any order not in opposition or in contravention of any decision of the Municipal Council.

The Chairperson ceases to hold office if he ceases to be a member of the Municipal Council. He may, by giving a notice in writing to the Vice-Chairperson or if there is no Vice-Chairperson, to the Council, resign his office. The Chairperson may be removed from office by a resolution carried by a majority of the total number of elected members of the Council at a special meeting called for this purpose. Such a meeting can be called upon a requisition made in writing by not less than one-third of the total number of elected members of the Council. However, no such resolution can be moved before the expiry of six months from the date of assumption of office by the Chairperson. In case of non-adoption of such a resolution, no further resolution for such purpose can be moved before the expiry of a period of six months from the date on which the former resolution was moved.

The Chairperson whose office becomes vacant continues to hold office as Chairperson until his successor enters upon his office.

Vice-Chairperson

The Vice-Chairperson, in the absence of the Chairperson, presides over the meetings of the Chairperson-in-Council as well as of the Municipal Council. He, during the absence of the Chairperson, the vice-chairperson discharges all the duties and exercises all the powers of the Chairperson. The Vice-Chairperson can perform such other duties or exercise such other powers as are delegated to him.

The Vice-Chairperson or any member of Chairperson-in-Council holds office until :

(a) he ceases to be a member of the Council, or
(b) he resigns his office by writing under his hand addressed to the Chairperson, or
(c) he is removed by written order of the Chairperson, or
(d) the Chairperson ceases to hold office, or
(e) in the case of death of the Chairperson, a newly elected Chairperson enters upon his office.

MUNICIPAL CORPORATION

A Municipal Corporation is the legislative body of the Municipality in larger urban area and all legislative actions are expressed to be made by the Corporation.

Mayor-in-Council

All executive powers of the Municipal Corporation vest in the Mayor-in-Council. It consists of the Mayor, the Deputy Mayor and the members not exceeding ten. The Mayor-in-Council is collectively responsible to the Corporation. All executive actions are expressed to be taken in the name of the Corporation. The Deputy Mayor and other members of the Mayor-in-Council are nominated by the Mayor from amongst the elected members of the Corporation.

Mayor

The Mayor is the executive head of the Municipal Corporation and the administration is under his control. He exercises all powers and discharges all functions as conferred on him. The Mayor presides at the meetings of the Mayor-in-Council and of the Corporation. The matters to be discussed in Mayor-in-Council are prepared under the direction of the Mayor and are circulated to the members of the Mayor-in-Council as he determines.

The Mayor-in-Council may authorize the Mayor in writing to take action in anticipation of its approval, sanction, consent or concurrence. Such an action has to be informed to the Mayor-in-Council. If the Mayor is satisfied that an emergency has arisen and is of the opinion that the immediate execution of any work for the doing of any act is necessary, he may direct the execution of such work without approval, sanction, consent or concurrence. He reports forthwith to the Corporation or to the Mayor-in-Council the action taken and the reasons thereof.

The elected members of the Corporation elect from amongst themselves at the first meeting of the Corporation one member to be Mayor. A Mayor ceases to hold office if he ceases to be member of the Corporation. He may, by giving notice in writing to the Corporation, resign his office. Such a resignation comes into effect from the date specified in the notice or from the date of its receipt by the Corporation. A Mayor may be removed from office by a resolution carried by a majority of total number of elected members at a special meeting called for the purpose upon a requisition made in writing by not less than one-third of the elected members of the Corporation. However, no such resolution can be moved before the expiry of six months from the date of assumption of office by a Mayor.

If such a resolution is not carried by majority of elected members of the Corporation, no further resolution for the removal of the Mayor can be moved before the expiry of a period of six months from the date on which the former was moved.

Deputy Mayor

The Deputy Mayor acts as Mayor in the event of the occurrence of any vacancy in the office of the Mayor. When the Mayor is unable to discharge his functions owing to absence, illness or any other cause, the Deputy Mayor discharges all his functions.

The Deputy Mayor or other members of the Mayor-in-Council holds office until he ceases to be a member of the Corporation or he resigns his office by writing under his hand addressed to the Mayor. The resignation comes into effect from the date of its acceptance. In case of the new Mayor entering upon his office the members cease to hold office.

Municipal Accounts Committee

A Municipal Corporation constitutes a Municipal Accounts Committee at its first meeting every year. The composition, powers, functions and the procedure of transacting business of the

Committee are prescribed under the rules framed by the State Government.

Disqualification of Members

A person can be disqualified for being chosen and for being a member of the Municipality, if he is disqualified by or under any law for the purpose of election to the State Legislature *or* he has directly or indirectly, by himself or by his partner or employer or employee, any share or interest in any contract or employment with, by, or on behalf of the Municipality *or* he is in the service or receives any remuneration from the Central, or the State Governments or the Municipality *or* has been elected to, or appointed under any other Municipality or any Panchayat institution *or* has been convicted by a criminal court punishable with imprisonment for a period of not less than ten years *or* has acquired any disqualification.

Election Petition

Any person qualified to vote may at any time within forty five days immediately after the declaration of the result, file a petition before the District Judge. Along with the petition, a security amount of Rs. 200 is required to be deposited. If the District Judge in setting aside the election, holds the candidate guilty of any corrupt practice, he may declare such candidate disqualified for contesting an election to a Municipality for a period not exceeding six years.

Transactions of Business

The Corporation/Council/Panchayat meets not less than once in every month for the transactions of business. The Mayor/ Chairperson can, upon requisition in writing by not less than one-third of the members, convene a meeting. All matters are decided by a majority of votes of the members present and voting.

The members of the Municipality may receive such remuneration or allowance as may be prescribed.

Municipal Officers

A Municipal Corporation or a Municipal Council has the following officers:

(a) A Municipal Secretary,
(b) An Executive Officer, and
(c) Such other officers and employees as may be prescribed. The Nagar Panchayat has the officers and employees as may be prescribed.

The officers and employees are appointed by the mayor/ Chairperson, however, the power to create or abolish any post vests in the State Government. The State Government after consultation with the Municipality may place the services of other officers also. A Municipality may avail the services of Engineers of the Public Works Department, Power, Minor Irrigation and Flood Control Departments of the State Government.

The State Government may, after consultation with the Municipality, transfer any officer or employee from one Municipality to another in public interest and for the betterment of the municipal administration.

Municipal Fund

Every Municipality constitutes a Municipal Fund to which all moneys received and realized by the Municipality are credited. All moneys credited to Municipal Fund are applied for payment of all sums, charges and costs necessary for carrying out the purposes of the Act.

Municipality may with the prior permission of the State Government obtain loan from any public financial institution.

Municipal Property

The Municipality has power to acquire by gift, purchase or otherwise and hold moveable and immoveable property within or outside the limit of the Municipal area. All public lands not belonging to Central or State Governments or statutory body, public tanks, streams, reservoirs and wells, public sewers, drains, channels, tunnels, culverts and water courses in, alongside or under any street, public streets and pavements, bus, taxi or rickshaw stands or other parkings or transportation terminals, stones and other materials thereof, and also trees on such public streets or pavements not belonging to any private individual, public *ghats* on rivers or streams or tanks, public parks and gardens, public lamps, lamp-posts and apparatus connected therewith, public places for disposal of the dead, all solid and liquid wastes collected on a public street or public place including dead animals and birds, and all stray animals not belonging to any private persons vest in the Municipality. The State Government may divest any property or transfer for a limited period for development and maintenance in the public interest.

The Municipality may dispose of any property by sale, lease or otherwise, let out, sell or transfer. However, prior permission of the State Government is required if value of the property exceeds certain amount as mentioned in the rules.

Every Municipality maintains an inventory and annual statement of moveable and immoveable properties in prescribed form and manner.

Powers, Functions and Duties

The Municipality is obliged to perform the functions and schemes envisaged in the Act. These are:

(i) To control all public streets, parkings, or transportation terminals, squares, parks and gardens vested in it;
(ii) Naming and numbering of streets and premises;
(iii) Lighting of streets and public places;
(iv) On its own or in collaboration with any one, erect plants for generation of electric power;
(v) Regulation or restriction of the use of sites for buildings;
(vi) Regulating building constructions;
(vii) Supply water for the use of inhabitants;
(viii) Construction and Maintenance of a system of drainage or sewerage as well, in a safe and sufficient manner in or outside the Municipal area;
(ix) Arrangements for collection, removal and disposal of solid wastes;
(x) Urban planning including town planning;
(xi) Planning for economic and social development;
(xii) Fire services,
(xiii) Urban forestry, protection of the environment and promotion of ecological aspects;
(xiv) Safeguarding the interests of weaker sections of society, including the handicapped and mentally retarded;

(xv) Slum improvement and upgradation;
(xvi) Promotion of cultural, educational and aesthetic aspects;
(xvii) Burials and burial grounds, cremation grounds, electric crematoriums;
(xviii) Cattle pounds, prevention of cruelty to animals;
(xix) Registration of slaughter houses and tanneries.

Taxes

A Municipality may levy, collect and appropriate following taxes, duties, tolls and fees:

(i) a property tax;
(ii) a tax on advertisement;
(iii) a tax on carts and carriages;
(iv) a toll on ferries and bridges;
(v) fees on licence and permit issued;
(vi) fees on construction or reconstruction of buildings, payable at the time of sanction of building plan;
(vii) fees on application filed;
(viii) fees for any specific service rendered by the Municipality;
(ix) a parking fee on vehicles; and
(x) a fee on the entry of vehicles and goods in the Municipal area.

Property Tax

Property tax consists of tax on lands and buildings and may include one or more of the following components:

(i) water tax,
(ii) sewerage tax,
(iii) conservancy tax,
(iv) lighting tax.

The property tax is charged on the basis of annual rental value. If the annual value of a holding is less than Rs. 200, the Municipality may exempt the owner for payment of property tax. The lands and buildings of the Central and State Governments, diplomatic office of foreign States, lands or building or portion thereof exclusively used for the purpose of public worship, public burial, *ghats* or sites used for disposal of the dead and open spaces including parade grounds are also exempted from the payment of property tax.

Recovery of Claims

If a person fails to make payment within the notified period, he can be penalized. On failure to pay property tax within a period of three months from the date when payment was due, the Municipality may take one or more of the following actions to enforce recovery of taxes:

(a) disconnect the water connection,

(b) request the power department of the State Government to discontinue power supply,

(c) file application in the court of judicial magistrate for realization of tax by issuing distress warrant for sale of moveable properties.

On failure to recover any sum from the owner, the amount may be recovered from the occupier of the lands or buildings and such occupier is entitled to reimbursement by the owner or adjustment against the rent payable by him.

In case of tax paid before the due date, the Municipality may grant rebate not exceeding ten per cent of the amount of tax.

Imposition of Taxes

The State Government may make rules to regulate the manner of levying the taxes. After assessment, every taxpayer is informed by the Municipality the amount of property tax and the time within which and the manner in which such tax is to be paid. Till the assessment is revised, the owner continues to pay the property tax without any further notice or intimation from the Municipality.

The Municipality notifies different dates and time for holding of different wards for payment of tax in the office. The Municipality may engage tax collectors on commission basis for collection of taxes and such tax collectors may be paid commission not exceeding ten per cent of the total amount of taxes collected by a tax collector.

Budget

The budget estimates are prepared and presented before a meeting of the Municipality, specially convened for the purpose, not later than the tenth day of March every year and is adopted within two weeks of presentation. A copy of the budget estimates is sent to the State Government. A revised budget is prepared and presented before the Municipality for adoption after the first day of October, but not later than thirty first day of December each year.

Accounts and Audit

A financial statement for the preceding year is prepared and presented within three months of the close of the year. Every Municipality prepares annually a balance sheet of assets and liabilities within six months of the close of the year.

The Municipal accounts are examined and audited by an auditor appointed by the State Government. The auditor submits the audit report to the Chairperson and a copy thereof to the State Government. The State Government may by rules provide for internal audit of the day-to-day accounts of a Municipality.

Municipal Police

With a view to implement the decisions of the Municipality in certain matters, a Municipality may, with the approval of the State Government, induct some police personnel from the State Police Organizations on deputation basis.

Rules and Regulations

The State Government may, by notification, makes rules for carrying out the provisions of the Act. The Municipality may make regulations.

Dissolution

The State Government, by order published in the Official Gazette stating the reason, may dissolve a Municipality if it has shown its incompetence to perform or has persistently made default in the performance of the duties imposed or has failed to carry out or implement the direction given by the State Government or has exceeded or abused its powers. The Municipality is given an opportunity of being heard before its dissolution which is laid before the State Legislature.

TRIBAL AREAS DISTRICT COUNCIL

The autonomous District Council for tribal areas is created for the purpose of self-government by the tribals in such areas. The State Government by notification in the Official Gazette, appoints a date on and from which there becomes an autonomous district comprising the tribal areas. The inclusion or exclusion of any area in the district may be made by the State Government only after consultation with the District Council.

There is a District Council for the Autonomous District. It is a body corporate and has perpetual succession and a common seal with power to acquire, hold and dispose of property. The Council may sue and be sued.

Composition

The District Council consists of 28 members who are elected on the basis of adult suffrage from territorial constituencies on single constituency basis. Three-fourths of the membership are reserved for Scheduled Tribes.

Election

A person is not qualified to be chosen as a member of a District Council unless he is an elector from any constituency. A person is disqualified for being chosen as or for being a member of the district Council if he is disqualified or becomes disqualified for being chosen as a member of either House of Parliament or holds any office of profit under the Central or State Government or the District Council.

The elected members of the Council hold office for a term of five years from the date appointed for the first meeting of the Council after the election, unless the Council is sooner dissolved. If the circumstances lead for holding of elections impracticable, the term may be extended by the Government for a period not exceeding one year at a time. A member elected to fill a casual vacancy holds office only for the remainder of term of the member whom he replaces.

An election to the District Council can be questioned only by an election petition before an authority not below the rank of District Judge, appointed by the State Government by notification.

Chairman and Vice-Chairman

The District Council has to choose two members to be respectively the Chairman and the Vice-Chairman. In case of any vacancy, the Council chooses another member to be Chairman or Vice-Chairman.

A member holding office as Chairman or Vice-Chairman of the Council vacates his office, if he ceases to be a member of the Council. He may be removed from his office by a resolution of the Council passed by not less than two-thirds of the members of the Council. A resolution to this effect can be moved only after a fourteen days notice has been given to move the resolution.

The Chairman may resign his office by writing under his hand addressed to the Vice-Chairman and the Vice-Chairman may resign by writing under his hand addressed to the Chairman.

Allowances

The Chairman and the Vice-Chairman are wholetime functionaries. They are entitled to such salaries and allowances as may be fixed by the State Government.

Every member is entitled to receive such allowances as may be fixed by the District Council in consultation with the State Government.

Executive Committee

Every District Council has an Executive Committee consisting of seven Executive members including the Chairman. The Chairman of the Council is the ex-officio Chairman of the Executive Committee. The Chairman as head of the Committee selects from and amongst the members of the District Council six persons to be the Executive members of the Committee. The members of the Committee may be paid such salaries and allowances as may be determined, by the District Council in consultation with the State Government.

The executive functions of the Council vest in the Executive Committee. Every order of the Committee is signed by the Chief Executive Officer or any other officer authorised in this behalf.

The Executive Committee disposes of all matters falling within its purview except cases involving any important change in the administrative system of the district or proposal for making resolutions, rules or bye-laws or cases which seriously affect or are likely to affect seriously the peace of good government or the Autonomous District or likely to affect relations with any such area or correspondences of importance with the Government and all important appointments.

Every member of the Committee is entrusted with specific subjects allocated by the Chairman. The Executive Committee is collectively responsible for all executive orders issued in the name of the District Council. One of the members is incharge of the District Fund, and he is in charge of the financial affairs of the District Council. The functions of the member-in-charge of the financial affairs are as under:

(i) He generally advises on all matters touching receipts and expenditure of the District Council.

(ii) He is responsible for all matters relating to financial procedures and the application of the principles of sound finance.

(iii) He prepares the budget of the Council and deals with all matters relating to budget procedure and the forms and contents of the financial statement.

(iv) He is responsible for the Ways and Means position of the District Fund.

Powers and Functions

The following matters within the area of the autonomous district fall under the exclusive control and administration of the District Council:

(i) The allotment, occupation or use or the setting apart of land, other than the reserved forest for the purpose of agriculture or grazing, or for residential or other non-agricultural purposes or for any other purpose likely to promote the interest of the inhabitants of any village, locality or town.

(ii) The management of any forest not being a reserved forest.

(iii) The use of any canal or water course for the purpose of agriculture.

(iv) The regulation of the practice of *Jhum* or other forms of shifting cultivation.

(v) The village or town committees or council.

(vi) Any other matter relating to village or town administration including village or town police and public health and sanitation.

In addition to above obligatory functions, the District Council may establish, construct or manage primary schools, dispensaries, markets, cattle pounds, ferries, fisheries, roads, road transport and waterways in the district. The Council may, with the previous approval of the Government, prescribe the language and the manner in which primary education be imparted.

The Government may, with the consent of the District Council, entrust to the Council or to its officers, functions in relation to agriculture, animal husbandry, community projects, cooperative societies, social welfare, village planning, fisheries and plantation or any other matter or which the executive power of the State extends.

Chief Executive Officer

There is a Chief Executive Officer in the District Council. He is appointed by the State Government and is paid out of the District Fund such salaries and allowances as are fixed by the Government.

The Chief Executive Officer is the principal executive officer of the District Council and all other officers and servants are subordinate to him. He is entitled to be present at a meeting of the District Council or of the Executive Committee or of any Committee established by the District Council and can take part in the discussions and with the consent of the Chairman or the president of the meeting. He may make a statement or explanation of facts but he is not entitled to vote or make any proposition. The Chief Executive Officer acts under the direction of the Chairman through whom he is responsible to the members of the Council.

The District Council may on resolution carried at a special meeting called for the purpose and supported by majority of the total number of members holding office request the State

Government for replacement of the Chief Executive Officer and the Government has to replace him. The Government may at any time withdraw from the District Council the officer appointed as Chief Executive Officer.

Taxes

The District Council has the power to collect within Autonomous District all or any of the taxes imposed under The Tripura Professions, Trades, Callings and Employment Taxations Act, 1976, The Tripura Land Revenue and Land Reforms Act, 1960 and the Bengal Agricultural Income Tax Act, 1944 as extended to the State of Tripura.

The District Council also has power to levy and collect all or any of the following fees:

(a) fees for the maintenance and development of schools, dispensaries or roads,
(b) fees on the entry of goods into a market, for sale therein and tolls on passengers and goods carried in ferries for maintenance and development thereof,
(c) fees on vehicles and boats for regulating and managing traffic,
(d) fees on animals at rate and in the manner as may be prescribed.

In addition, a share of the royalties accruing each year from forest, licence or lease for the purposes of prospecting for, or the extraction of minerals granted by the Government in respect of area within the Autonomous District is made over to the District Council. The share is agreed upon between the Government and the Council. In case of any dispute, the matter is referred to an arbitrator appointed by the Government for determination and the amount determined is deemed to be the amount payable to the Council. The decision of the arbitrator is final.

Administration of Justice

The Government may constitute village councils within the autonomous district to the exclusion of any court and may appoint in consultation with the Chairman and failing him the Vice-Chairman of the District Council, suitable persons to be members or presiding officers of village councils. The Government may also appoint officers for the administration of the bye-laws and regulations made by the District Council.

The village councils have power to try falling civil suits if their values do not exceed one thousand rupees:

(i) civil suits for money due on contract,
(ii) civil suits for recovery of property or for the value thereof,
(iii) civil suits for compensation for wrongfully taking or injuring any property,
(iv) civil suits for damages caused by cattle trespass.

The village council has power to try cases or offences of the following description and to impose fine not exceeding three hundred rupees:

(i) cases arising out of any bye-laws, regulations or rules in force in the autonomous district,
(ii) cases arising out of any bye-laws, regulations offences or abatement thereof which are not punishable with death, imprisonment for life or imprisonment for a term not exceeding six months and offences under the Indian Penal Code where the value of the stolen property does not exceed five hundred rupees.

In case of civil suits an, appeal can lie to the District Judge against final decision of the village council and as regards latter cases an appeal can be made to the Sessions Judge. If any fine or portion thereof remains unpaid, the same be deemed to be due to the Government and can be realized as arrears of land revenue.

District Council Fund

All moneys received by the District Council in course of administration of district are credited to the District Fund. The Government may make rules for the management of the District Fund and for the procedure to be followed in respect of payment of money into the Fund, withdrawal of moneys, the custody of moneys and any other related matters.

The accounts of the District Council is kept in the form prescribed by the Government. The audit of the accounts is entrusted by the State Government to the Comptroller and Auditor General of India who may submit the report to the Government. The Government transmits the report to the

District Council for discussion and consideration. The Council returns the report to the Government with comments and the Government, in turn lays report with the comment of the Council before the State Legislature.

Property

All properties of the nature specified below and situated in the autonomous district vest in and belong to the District Council with all other properties which may become vested in the Council and be under the direction, management and control of the District Council:

(a) all public buildings constructed and maintained out of the fund of the District Council,

(b) all public roads, which have been constructed or maintained out of the fund of the Council and the stones and other materials, implements and things provided for such roads,

(c) all lands or other properties, movable or immovable, transferred to the Council by the Government.

Budget

Estimated receipts and expenditure of an autonomous district ending 31st March of every year is first placed before the District Council for discussion and then transmitted to the Government by the 31st January of the preceding year.

Conduct of Business

The District Council meets for the conduct of business at least once in every six months. The council conducts its business in the name and the procedure presented by the Government.

Officers and Staff

The District Council may appoint officers and staff necessary for the administration of the bye-laws and rules or regulations made by it and also for the proper and efficient execution of its duties.

Rules, Bye-Laws and Regulations

The Government may make rules for the provisions of the Act. Every rule made is laid before the Legislative Assembly. The Government may make rules relating to:

(i) composition of village councils and the number of village councils and defining their territorial limits within the district,
(ii) the procedure regarding cognizance by village councils,
(iii) the procedure to be followed by the village councils in the trial of suits, cases or offences,
(iv) all other ancillary matters.

The District Council may make rules for the regulation and control of money lending or trading within the district. It may :

(a) prescribe that no one except the holder of a licence issued in that behalf, can carry on the business of money lending,
(b) prescribe the maximum rate of interest which may be charged or be recovered by a moneylender,
(c) provide for the maintenance of accounts by money-lenders and for inspection of such accounts by officers appointed by the District Council.

All regulations come into effect upon their publication in the Official Gazette.

The District Council has power to frame bye-laws in respect to:

(i) inheritance to property of persons belonging to Scheduled Tribes,
(ii) marriage and divorce where any of the parties to the marriage belongs to Scheduled Tribes,
(iii) all matters relating to the functions entrusted to it.

The bye-laws come into effect upon their publication in the Official Gazette.

Control

The Government may appoint a Commission to examine and report on any matter relating to the administration of the autonomous district and particularly on the following:

(i) the provisions of educational and medical facilities and communication in autonomous district,
(ii) the need for any new or special legislation in respect of the autonomous district,
(iii) the administration of bye-laws, rules and regulations.

The report of the Commission with recommendations of the

Government is laid before the legislature together with an explanatory Memorandum regarding the actions proposed to be taken.

If at any time, the Government is satisfied that a bye-law or regulation or resolution or rule of the District Council is likely to endanger the safety and security of the State or is likely to be prejudicial to public order, the State Government may annul or suspend such bye-law, rule, resolution and take necessary steps.

Dissolution

The Government may, on the recommendation of the Commission, by notification in the Official Gazette, order the dissolution of the District Council. It may direct that a fresh general election be held immediately for the reconstitution of the Council, simultaneously the Government may place the administration of the autonomous district under the Commission or any other body considered suitable for a period not exceeding twelve months.

LIST OF TOWNS

Name of Town	*Population (1991)*	*Growth Rate (1971-81)*	*1981-91)*
1. Agartala City	1,57,636	31.84	19.25
2. Badharghat	35,082	-	-
3. Teliamura	27,663	-	-
4. Jogendranagar	26,961	-	-
5. Dharmanagar	25,898	23.42	24.47
6. Udaipur	18,222	17.09	11.76
7. Kailasahar	16,166	22.03	24.95
8. Kumarghat	14,640	-	-
9. Barjala	14,583	-	-
10. Pratapgarh	13,881	-	-
11. Belonia	13,268	5.98	10.07
12. Khawai	12,553	14.82	17.08
13. Singerbil	9,160	-	-
14. Amarpur	8,548	-	19.55
15. Sonamura	8,135	-	27.51
16. Gandhigram	7,524	-	-
17. Sabroma	4,763	-	42.60
18. Kamalpur	4,300	-	16.59

Appendices

TABLE - 1
COMPOSITION OF MUNICIPALITIES

State	*Transitional Area*	*Smaller Urban Area*	*Larger Urban Area*
Assam	Nagar Panchayat or Town Committee	Municipal Board	Municipal Corporation
Manipur	Nagar Panchayat	Municipal Council	Municipal Corporation
Tripura	Nagar Panchayat (Pop. below 50,000)	Municipal Council (Pop. 50,000-5 lakhs)	Municipal Corporation (Pop. 5 lakhs and more)
Sikkim	Nagar Panchayat	Municipal Council	—

TABLE - 2
MEMBERS AND CHAIRPERSONS

State	*Name of Members*	*Name of Chairman*	*Term*	*Mode of Election*
Assam	Commissioner	Chairman		Indirect
Manipur	Councillor	Chairperson	Co-terminus	Indirect
Tripura	Member	Chairperson		Indirect
Sikkim	Member	Chairperson/ Sabhapati		Indirect

TABLE - 3
CONSTITUTION OF MUNICIPALITIES

States	*Nagar Panchayats*			*Municipalities*			*Municipal Corporation*		
	Elected	*Ex-Officio*	*Nominated/ Appointed*	*Elected*	*Ex-Officio*	*Nominated/ Appointed*	*Elected*	*Ex-Officio*	*Nominated Appointed*
Assam	Determined by the State Government			10-13	MPs, MLAs, Chairmen of Wards Committees	Appointed members as experts	60	MPs, MLAs, Chairmen of Wards Committees	Experts
Manipur	Determined by the State Government		one	Determined by the State Government		one			
Meghalaya	As in Assam								
Tripura	5-15	Chairperson of Wards Committees	two	15-20	Chairperson of Wards Committees	three	20-40	Chairperson of Wards Committees	Five
Sikkim	Elected Members			3-9	MPs, MLAs	one expert			

TABLE-4
RESERVATION

State	*Scheduled Castes*	*Scheduled Tribes*	*Backward Classes*	*Women*
Assam	Proportion in Population	Proportion in Population	—	One-third
Manipur	Proportion in Population	Proportion in Population	—	One-third
Tripura	Proportion in Population	Proportion in Population	—	One-third
Sikkim	Proportion in Population	Proportion in Population	—	One-third

TABLE-5
NUMBER OF FUNCTIONS

State	*Nagar Panchayat*		*Municipal Council*		*Municipal Corporation*	
	Mandatory	*Discretionary*	*Mandatory*	*Discretionary*	*Mandatory*	*Discretionary*
Assam	13	25	13	25	24	47
Manipur	21	20	21	20	—	—
Tripura	19	—	19	—	—	—
Sikkim	18	—	18	—	—	—

TABLE-6
FUNCTIONS OF SCHEDULE XII

State	*Nagar Panchayat*		*Municipal Council*		*Municipal Corporation*	
	Mandatory	*Discretionary*	*Mandatory*	*Discretionary*	*Mandatory*	*Discretionary*
Assam	Not included clearly	—	—	—	—	5
Manipur	Not included clearly	—	—	—	—	—
Tripura	9	—	9	—	—	—
Sikkim	18	—	18	—	—	—

TABLE-7
NUMBER OF TAXES

State	*Nagar Panchayat*		*Municipal Council*		*Municipal Corporation*	
	Obligatory	*Optional*	*Obligatory*	*Optional*	*Obligatory*	*Optional*
Assam	—	15	—	15	6	9
Manipur	—	12	—	12		
Tripura	—	10	—	10	—	10
Sikkim	—	18	—	18	—	—

TABLE-8
DISTRICT PLANNING COMMITTEE

State	*Constitution*	*Chairman*	*Remarks*
Assam	MPs, MLAs, President of Zilla Parishad, Mayor or Chairperson of Municipal Corporation/Municipal Board/Town Committee having jurisdiction over the headquarter of the District, 4/5 members elected	President of Zilla Parishad	CEO of the Zilla Parishad is Secretary Deputy Commissioner is permanent invitee as ex-officio
Manipur	Members of Lok Sabha, MLAs, Adhyaksha of Zilla Parishad, Mayor/ President, 4/5 members elected	Deputy Commissioner	Chairman of District Cooperative Bank as permanent invitee CEO is Secretary
Tripura	Details not mentioned		
Sikkim	MPs, Adhyaksha of Zilla Panchayat, Chairperson of Municipalities, 4/5 elected	Adhyaksha of Zilla Panchayat	District Development Officer is Member Secretary MLAs, District Collector, District Development Officer-cum-Panchayat Officer permanent invitee

TABLE-9
WARDS COMMITTEE

State	*Composition*	*Members*	*Functions*	*Remarks*
Assam	Not more than four wards	4 Ward members 4 Nominated citizens	Look after the needs of residents	Chairman elected indirectly
Manipur	Not less than five wards	One officer acts as Secretary Executive Officer ex-officio member	Prescribed by rules	Chairperson elected by the elected members from amongst themselves
Tripura	Details not given			
Sikkim	No mention			

TABLE-10
STATE FINANCE COMMISSION

State	*Constitution*	*Election of Members/ Chairperson*
Assam	4 Members including Chairman	As may be prescribed
Manipur	Constituted under the Manipur Panchayati Raj Act, 1994	
Tripura	Details not given	
Sikkim	Provision made in the Act	

TABLE-11
STATE ELECTION COMMISSION

State	*Constitution*	*President*	*Remarks*
Assam	Mentioned in the definition section of the Act		
Manipur	Constituted under the Manipur Panchayat Raj Act, 1994		
Tripura	Details not given		
Sikkim	Provision made in the Act		

TABLE-12
PARTICULARS OF TAXES

Taxes	*Assam*			*Manipur*		*Tripura*		*Sikkim*	
	Nagar Pancha-yat	*Muni-cipal Council*	*Muni-cipal Corpo-ration*	*Nagar Pancha-yat*	*Muni-cipal Council*	*Nagar Pancha-yat*	*Muni-cipal Council*	*Nagar Pancha-yat*	*Muni-cipal Council*
(1)	(2)	(3)	(4)	(5)	(6)	(7)	(8)	(9)	(10)
i) Taxes on Lands and Buildings	D	D	M	D	D	D	D	D	D
ii) Octroi	—	—	D	D	D	D	D	D	D
iii) Stamp Duty	—	—	M	D	D	—	—	D	D
iv) Tax on Professions	—	—	M	—	—	—	—	D	D
v) Tax on Vehicle	—	—	M	D	D	D	D	D	D
vi) Tax on Animals	D	D	M	D	D	—	—	D	D
vii) Tax on Dogs	D	D	D	—	—	—	—	D	D
viii) Show Tax	—	—	M	—	—	—	—	D	D
ix) Toll	D	D	D	—	—	D	D	D	D
x) Tax on Boats/Ferries	D	D	D	—	—	D	D	—	—
xi) Tax on Electricity	—	—	—	—	—	—	—	—	—
xii) Pilgrimage Fee	—	—	D	—	—	—	—	D	D
xiii) Drainage Fee	D	D	D	D	D	—	—	D	D
xiv) Lighting Fee	D	D	—	D	D	—	—	D	D

(1)	*(2)*	*(3)*	*(4)*	*(5)*	*(6)*	*(7)*	*(8)*	*(9)*	*(10)*
xv) Scavenging Fee	—	—	—	D	D	—	—	—	—
xvi) Latrine Fee	—	—	—	D	D	D	D	D	D
xvii) Fee on Service	—	—	—	—	—	D	D	—	—
xviii) Tax on Servants	—	—	—	—	—	—	—	—	—
xix) Tax on Building	—	—	—	—	—	D	D	—	—
Applications									
xx) Tax on Advertisement	—	—	M	—	—	D	D	D	D
xxi) Fee on Licence	—	—	—	D	D	D	D	—	—
xxii) Parking Fee	—	—	—	—	—	D	D	—	—
xxiii) Water Tax	D	D	—	—	—	—	—	—	—
xxiv) Tax on Private Markets	D	D	—	D	D	—	—	D	D
xxv) Fee on Fire Brigade	D	D	—	D	D	—	—	—	—
xxvi) Fee on Health Services	D	D	—	—	—	—	—	—	—
xxvii) Betterment Tax	—	—	D	—	—	—	—	D	D

M - Mandatory; D - Discretionary

Index